WHIRLIGIGS & WEATHERVANES

Whirligig carved by Parks Townsend,
Elizabethton, Tennessee

Editing: Thom Boswell
Design & Production: Thom Boswell
Typesetting: Elaine Thompson
Photography: Evan Bracken
Instructional Drawings: Houston Hammond
   & Don Osby

Library of Congress Cataloging-in-Publication Data
Schoonmaker, David.
   Whirligigs and weather vanes : a celebration of wind gadgets
with dozens of creative projects to make / David Schoonmaker
& Bruce Woods.
      p.   cm.
   "A Sterling/Lark book."
   Includes index.
   ISBN 0-8069-8364-7
   1. Wooden toy making.   2. Whirligigs.   3. Weathervanes.
I. Woods, Bruce, 1947-   .   II. Title.
TT174.5.W6S34   1991
745.592--dc20   91-12145
                                    CIP

10 9 8 7

A Sterling/Lark Book

Produced by Altamont Press, Inc.
50 College Street, Asheville, NC 28801

First paperback edition published in 1992 by
Sterling Publishing Company, Inc.
   387 Park Avenue South, New York, N.Y. 10016

© 1991 by Altamont Press
Text © 1991 by David Schoonmaker & Bruce Woods

Distributed in Canada by Sterling Publishing
% Canadian Manda Group, P.O. Box 920, Station U
   Toronto, Ontario, Canada M8Z 5P9
Distributed in Great Britain and Europe by
Cassell PLC
   Villiers House, 41/47 Strand, London WC2N
   5JE, England
Distributed in Australia by Capricorn Link Ltd.
   P.O. Box 665, Lane Cove, NSW 2066

Printed in China

Sterling   ISBN 0-8069-8364-7   Trade
                 0-8069-8365-5   Paper

WHIRLIGIGS & WEATHERVANES

A Celebration of Wind Gadgets

with Dozens of Creative Projects To Make

David Schoonmaker & Bruce Woods

A Sterling/Lark Book

Sterling Publishing Co., Inc.   New York

TABLE OF CONTENTS

"Channel Swimmer"
by Edward "Rainbow" Larson,
Santa Fe, New Mexico

INTRODUCTION

Whirligigs and weathervanes: as American as...the House of Lords? True, though both of these folk art forms have become almost synonymous with Americana, they were happily spinning their windy magic in Europe long before westward breezes shouldered the Mayflower toward these shores.

Nonetheless, few would argue that both the whirligig and the weathervane reached the pinnacles of the folk art world at the hands of early American craftspeople, for whom such simple constructions provided an inexpensive outlet for creative energies, yielding attractive but practical helpmates around the house and garden, and even gifts to delight the young and young at heart.

Today, you'll not find many whirligig builders listed in your local Yellow Pages—or even displaying their wares at craft shows. A pity. But the *amateur* folk art of whirligig building is actually thriving.

These new builders, mindful of tradition but imbued with a slightly rebellious spirit, are turning their handiwork toward contem-

Biplane whirligig by
unknown artist in Texas

porary expressions. Take the Tennessee minister, for example, who populated the hillside behind his home with a sometimes-R-rated gallery of whirligigs depicting decades of his town's juiciest scandals.

We, too, are mindful of tradition, but, as you might have guessed from the whirligigs that grace our cover, we, too, have followed the prevailing winds into uncharted territory. It might be a traditional theme—the mermaid windvane—but there's a little edge of individuality to her. Or it might be a traditional pastime—the duck hunter in his boat—rendered with untraditional reciprocating motion. But, by the time you thumb back to our "Cat House," we think you'll agree that tradition is strictly optional.

Here you'll find whirligig hummingbirds that hover over waiting flowers, spinning-winged lawn decorations to make the most brazen flamingo hide its head, and Rube Goldberg contraptions that take the capabilities of wooden figures and bent-wire cams to their very limits.

But most important of all, we don't want you to stop there. Build a whirligig or two, mount a weathervane, and your own creative fires may well be blown into life. The pages that follow will supply all of the basics of lever and pivot, of bushing and mount. Learn them and play with them. After all, though the "wind toy" story is an old one, new chapters are being written every day. They're written by playful minds and nimble hands, and their muse is a playful breeze.

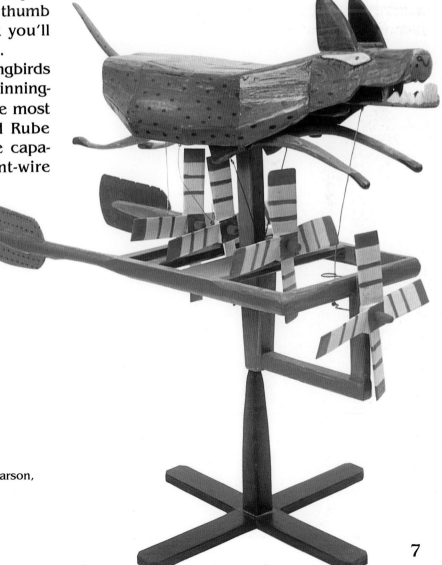

"Drum Major" (left) by John Butner, Bethania, North Carolina (ca. 1940); two tiny bellows actually whistle through organ pipes.

"Doberman Pincer" by Edward "Rainbow" Larson, Santa Fe, New Mexico

Whence came the whirligig? Frankly, no one knows, but it's fairly easy, and entertaining, to speculate. These fascinating wind toys, at least in the form we've come to recognize, are defined by a variety of interacting forms of motion. They spin (as does a pinwheel or propeller), they turn on their bases (like a weathercock or windvane), and they move upon swivels and axles to perform their eternal dances (taking their lead from puppets and a wide variety of moving toys). Each of these distinctive actions has a mechanism and a history of its own. And so, strictly speaking, the whirligig has not one genealogy but three.

The oldest ancestor of today's whirligig is almost certainly the windvane. Even the most primitive of human societies had reason to keep track of the direction of the wind. Changing breezes can give warning of the turning of the weather (hence the term weathervane), presaging rain or drought, and can even, in some areas with especially strong seasonal prevailing winds, accurately clock the great, slow turnings of the year. The simplest of weathervanes were likely little more than flags of hide, grass, animal hair or feathers.

Mankind's great urge to replicate must have soon exerted its influence, though, and, with the boring of a shallow socket and the installation of a spindle of antler-point, the simple flag became a totem carving, a bird or beast that would point out the direction from which the changing weather approached. The origin of the Western windvane is lost in our prehistory. Interestingly enough, the venerable Oxford English Dictionary (the OED) lists neither "windvane" nor "weathervane." It does, however, cite references to "weathercock" going back to 1300 A.D. "Whirligig", as we'll see, goes back—in various spelling guises—almost as far.

"Witch on a Broomstick" by unknown artist, New England (ca. 1870); from the permanent collection of The Museum of American Folk Art, gift of Dorothy & Leo Rabkin

If the whirligig was born of the pivoting windvane, however, it only reached its maturity with the addition of one form or another of pinwheel or propeller. In fact, the combination of pinwheel and pivoting base pretty much forms the definition for the simplest of the whirligigs of today.

And as you might imagine, the origins of the propeller are about as hard to pin down as those of mankind itself. It's a safe guess that the earliest pinwheels took their inspiration from the airfoils found in nature. There are ready models to learn from, such as the helicoptering seed pods of trees and the stiff flight and tail feathers of birds.

"Archangel Gabriel" by unknown artist, American (1840); from the permanent collection of the Museum of American Folk Art, gift of Adele Earnest

9

Although this thought may go against some of our most dearly held misconceptions, our earliest ancestors were great learners and innovators. Their abilities to observe the world around them, and to profit from such observation, were their greatest tools. Thus the stone-age aboriginal people in Australia observed, it's speculated, a peculiarly bent seedpod and made the great leap of intuition that resulted in the returning boomerang (a propeller!), the physics of which are providing food for learned scientific papers to this day.

"Mermaid" by unknown artist, Wayland, Massachusetts (ca. 1850); Shelburne Museum, Shelburne, Vermont

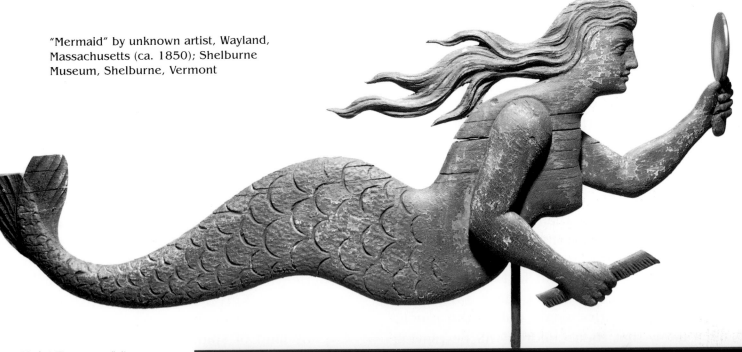

"Saint Tammany" (top left) by unknown artist, East Branch, New York (ca. 1850); from the permanent collection of The Museum of American Folk Art, gift of Effie Thixton Arthur

"Black Hawk Horse" (bottom left) weathervane attributed to Henry Leach (1871); National Museum of American Art, Smithsonian Institution, gift of H. W. Hemphill, Jr.

"Whirligig with Two Figures" (right) by un-known artist (ca. 1900); National Museum of American Art, Smithsonian Institution, gift of H. W. Hemphill, Jr.

11

A WHIRL THROUGH HISTORY

Some researchers guess that the pinwheel travelled west from China as a primitive windmill, arriving in Europe sometime in the 12th century. (The OED finds its first reference to "windmill" in 1297, but it's reasonably certain that they were spinning long before that.) Since the evidence is open to interpretation, it's really anybody's guess. We prefer to believe that the simple spinner impressed its magic on many world cultures independently. (In fact, should some science-fiction apocalypse leave a new race of humans to rise again out of the muck, it's likely that their children will be playing with pinwheels before the adults discover a means of making fire!)

And once you have a wind-spinner, it doesn't take much inspiration to want to let it pivot to face the wind. Voila. The whirligig is born. Of course, over the years these simple toys learned a few other tricks, as many of them became tiny stages upon which whittled thespians continuously strutted their simple plays. And these tiny actors and actresses have histories of their own.

Among the most primitive of known manipulated figurines are those of ancient Egypt. Emanuel Hercik, in his history of playthings *(Les Jouets Populaires)*, illustrates a "grinding corn" doll, activated by a string, that uses virtually the same pivot and balance points as such comparatively modern whirligigs as the washerwoman and the woodchopper...yet this toy probably amused the children of the Pharaohs! Pull-toys are another likely means through which these figures were developed, with the turning of the wheels providing the action. Early push-pull toys—which had two handles, each one held by a child, that caused their figures to perform as the sticks were pushed and pulled by the children—also illustrate some themes very familiar to today's whirligig fancier. Hercik's book includes drawings of such toys designed upon several variations on a Middle Eastern fairy tale theme, in which a blacksmith and a bear take alternating whacks at an anvil.

The oldest Western reference to "whyrlegyge," again taken from the OED, was in 1440. It's not known, however, when the word evolved from simply meaning any kind of spinning toy to the specific definition it enjoys today. The earliest European records of true whirligigs date back to the 18th century. It's safe to say that these simple toys reached the New World with its first colonists—possibly before. Consider the long days at sea that were part and parcel of those early voyages of discovery, and the calming effect that whittling is known to have upon a mind that may well be worried about sailing off the edge of the world!

From colonial America, through westward expansion, the industrial revolution, and into our technological age, the whirligig has evolved as a truly American folk art, respecting its heritage, but always eager to learn and to profit from the developments surrounding it.

In that spirit, we offer these many diverse examples of whirligigs and weathervanes for your amusement and inspiration—from the most primitive to the unashamedly modern. And after learning to build a few of our designs, perhaps you'll make your own original contribution to this art form, becoming a true whirligigger in the ongoing tradition of "Air Americana."

"Spinning Woman Whirligig,"
Shelburne Museum,
Shelburne, Vermont

"Uncle Sam Riding a Bicycle" by unknown artist, Northeastern United States (1880-1920); from the permanent collection of The Museum of American Folk Art, promised bequest of Dorothy & Leo Rabkin

"Early Bird Gets the Worm" attributed to Jack Mongillo, Salamanca, New York (ca. 1920); from the permanent collection of The Museum of American Folk Art, promised bequest of Dorothy & Leo Rabkin

"Hula Dancer" attributed to an American soldier in Hawaii (ca. 1940); Old Orchard Antiques, Asheville, North Carolina

"Whirligig with Witch and Horse" (left) by Charlie Burnham (1918); National Museum of American Art, Smithsonian Institution, gift of H. W. Hemphill, Jr.

A CONTEMPORARY GALLERY

"Wind Machine with Gabriel, Eleanor Roosevelt, and Louis Armstrong"
by James Leonard (1984); National Museum of American Art,
Smithsonian Institution, gift of H. W. Hemphill, Jr.

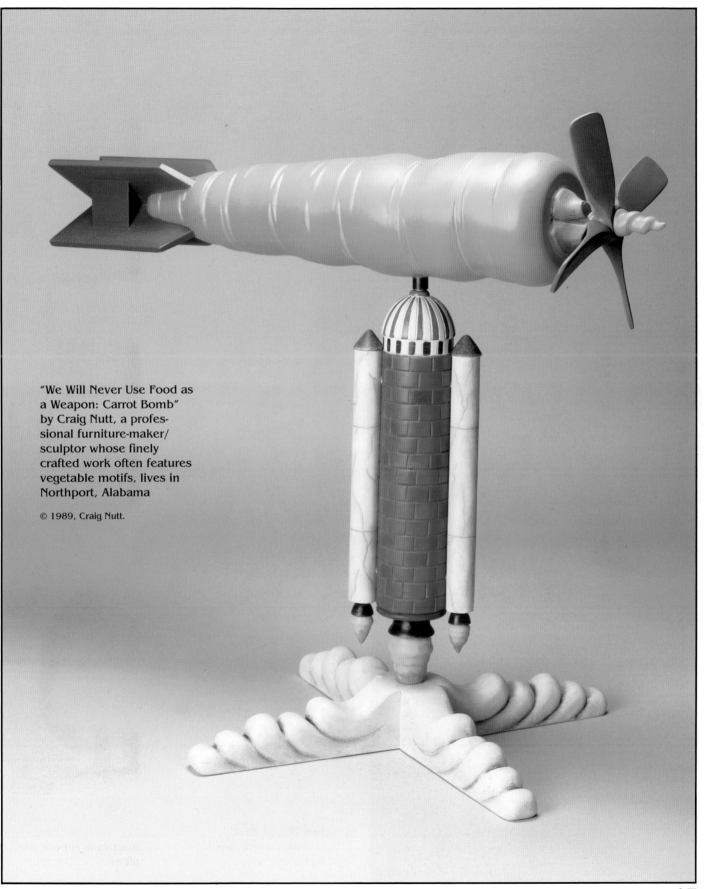

"We Will Never Use Food as a Weapon: Carrot Bomb" by Craig Nutt, a professional furniture-maker/ sculptor whose finely crafted work often features vegetable motifs, lives in Northport, Alabama

© 1989, Craig Nutt.

"Killer Whale" weathervane by Randy Sewell, a whirligig enthusiast who also makes fanciful bird houses and stained glass in Atlanta, Georgia

"Pig Rowing" whirligig by Randy Sewell

"White Sea Bass" complex windvane by Randy Sewell

18

"Chorus Line" by Anders Lunde,
Somerhill Gallery, Chapel Hill,
North Carolina

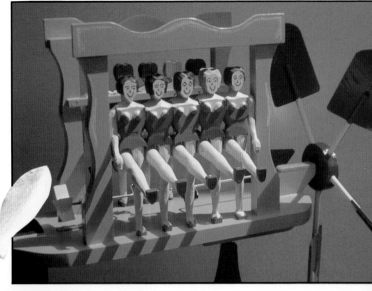

"Fish" whirligig
by Anders Lunde

"Sailboats" whirligig (below) by Magella Normand,
Gaspé, Quebec, Canada

"Sailboats" whirligig by P. E. LeBatard (b. 1886)
Gautier, Mississippi; the sails can be heard to pop
in a strong wind as they tack and rotate.

These delightful wind toys
are made by T. R. Reed,
Tuscaloosa, Alabama

"Mixed Doubles,"
T. R. Reed

"Anthony and Cleopatra,"
T. R. Reed

"Montezuma,"
T. R. Reed

"Jitterbugs,"
T. R. Reed

"Flying Dutchman,"
T. R. Reed

"Computowoman,"
T. R. Reed

"Venus on the Halfshell,"
T. R. Reed

"Chicken o' the Sea,"
T. R. Reed

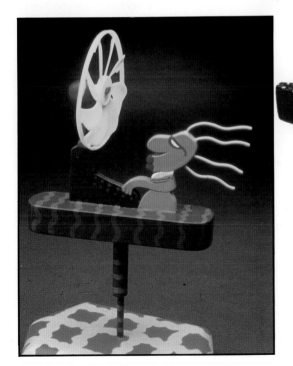

These highly stylized whirligigs are
crafted by Ann Wood and Dean Lucker,
St. Paul, Minnesota

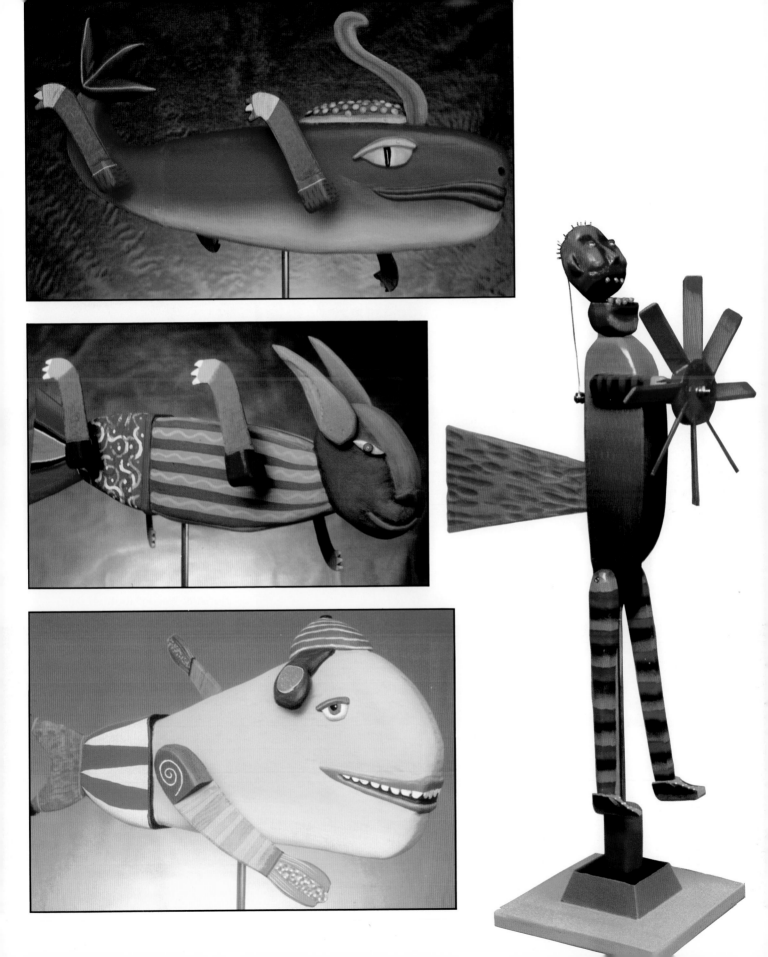

James Harold Jennings (b. 1932), an authentic rustic character "inspired by electroencephalography and metempsychosis," obsessively crafts his primitive creations from raw timber and found objects in the rural piedmont of North Carolina.

"Indians in War Canoe" (below)

"Three Men in a Sub" (right)

"Floppy Ladies" (top right)

"Elvis" whirligig (middle right)

"Fiddlers" (bottom left, opposite)

"Horse & Wagon" (bottom right)

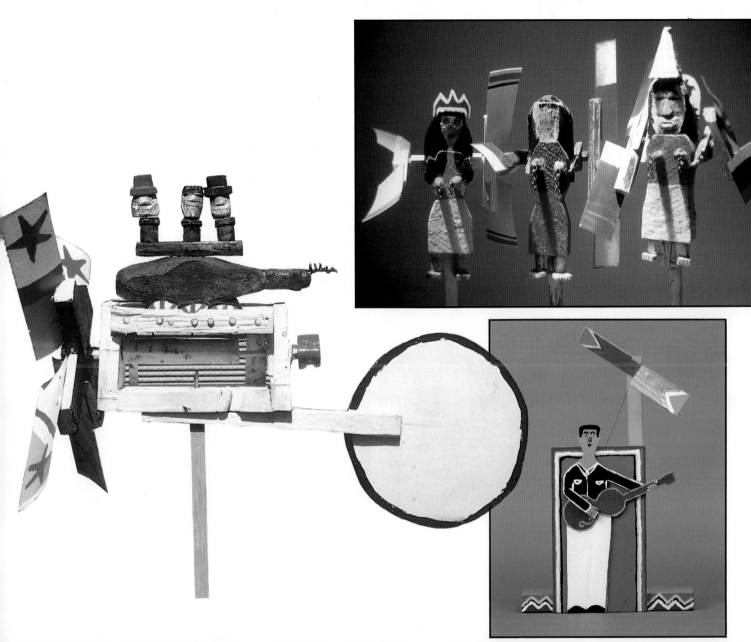

Vollis Simpson (b. 1919) constructs his huge metal wind sculptures in Lucama, North Carolina. They tower up to forty feet, and are covered with light reflectors that produce a night-time spectacle.

27

Edward "Rainbow" Larson, formerly of Washington Island, Wisconsin, now fashions his often politically inspired whirligigs in Santa Fe, New Mexico. His work is as elaborate as it is entertaining.

Represented by The Elaine Horwitch Gallery, Santa Fe

"U.S. Missile System" (right)

"U.S. Space Shuttle" (below)

"Right to Machine" (bottom right)

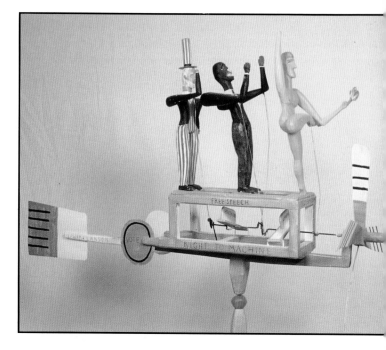

28

"1957 Chrysler (Nixon, Big Business, American Public)"

"Ronald Reagan Strikes Out on Foreign Policy"

"World Car We All Ride In"

"Full Employment/Walking the Dog
(a commentary on social stratification)"

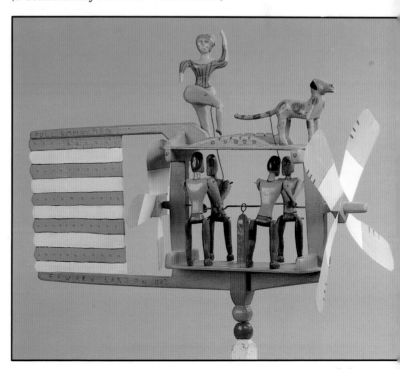

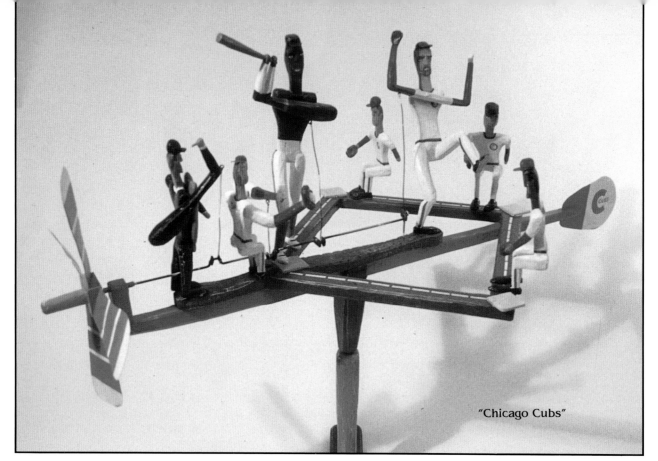

"Chicago Cubs"

"Chicago Bears"

30

"The Golden Arches"

"Duke Ellington & His Band, Billie Holiday Singing"

31

CONSTRUCTION TECHNIQUES

Within the universe of woodworking, whirligigs and windvanes are relatively tame. For the most part, they depict—and even animate—their subjects in profile, so the shaping is generally two-dimensional. Depth, or the perception of it, is accomplished either by simply adding layers or with paint.

In exchange for this simplicity, some of these projects require other skills. The mechanical linkages in the whirligigs add an element of metalwork—though nothing especially demanding or requiring expensive tools. Also, artful painting can take an otherwise mundane shape and render it life-like.

In fact, we'd suggest that the joy—and challenge—of building whirligigs and windvanes is this very marriage of different skills. For the woodworker who's accustomed to working objects that are monolithic—or, at most, moving at right angles—dealing with parts that move in arcs and at varying angles can be mind-expanding. It requires a retraining of the eye to visualize what effect a cam and its connecting rod may have on the motion of a part. Likewise, paint detail and blending will show the woodworker new dimensions of familiar materials.

MATERIALS

A windvane or whirligig could be—and probably has been—made of most anything. But we can narrow the field considerably by concentrating on materials that are easy to work with *and* durable. That makes wood the natural choice.

You could build your wind toy from any weather-resistant standard-size lumber that pleases you—with one proviso. Because boards come in a limited selection of thick-nesses, your choice of stock will affect the overall scale of the project. If you settle on standard 1-by lumber, for example, and the design calls for three layers, it will be 2-1/4" inches thick—a substantial piece.

Plywood offers a more extensive selection of thicknesses than solid boards, not to mention a convenient set of multiples. The laminar lumber is commonly available in 1/4", 3/8", 1/2", 5/8" and 3/4" thicknesses, so you have the luxury of combining 1/4", 1/2" and 3/4", for example, to achieve special effects. Further, if you want a larger or smaller overall size than we show in this book, you can use a different scale material and adjust the linear dimensions accordingly.

That said, there are instances where there's no substitute for the workable grain of a good hardwood board. Throughout the text we'll note what material we used and why, and the following comments will give you some room to substitute according to local availability.

PICKING PLYWOOD

At the minimum, you want to use exterior-grade plywood; its water-resistant glue prevents delamination when exposed to the elements. Grade will depend on the particular project and your budget, but here are some general guidelines.

Plywood is graded by the quality of the faces: either A, B, C or D. Thankfully, there is no F—yet. The material will be stamped with a hyphenated two-letter combination, and may have a suffix describing its application. C-DX, for example, has one C face, one D face and glue suited to exterior applications. In this case, neither face is anything close to lovely; C-DX usually goes under shingles.

In a multi-layer project, you may be able to get away with one A-grade face on the outside and a lesser grade (commonly C) facing in. More often, you'll want at least A-B plywood, and, to be honest, it's neither easy to find nor cheap. (Incidentally, don't be distracted by the pretty birch- or oak-veneer plywoods at the building supply. They're made for indoor cabinets and won't last long outside.)

Unless you're planning to go into mass production and material costs are crucial, we suggest you ask for marine plywood. By its name, you've already guessed that it's very durable. It has other advantages, as well. First, marine plywood has no voids—knot holes between the layers that don't show until you cut into a sheet. Second, because boat builders need thin, strong sheets, it's stiffer than equivalent-thickness exterior plywood. And finally, both faces are of good quality.

If you live in an area with lots of boating, marine plywood may be readily available. Otherwise, you'll have to ask your lumberyard to get a sheet for you. They'll probably be aware of what it is, and should be able to get it fairly quickly. They may offer pressure-treated plywood as a substitute. It's just regular exterior plywood that's had chromated copper arsenates applied to make it last in severe applications. You don't really need pressure-treated plywood, and the residues on its surface prevent it from taking paint well. We suggest you stand your ground and go with marine.

In the materials lists that will accompany each project, we won't specify a particular type of plywood. Let your pocket book be your guide.

STANDARD LUMBER

Some projects do specify solid (that is, nonlaminated) lumber for certain parts. There are a number of choices, but there are some fairly specific criteria for our projects that narrow the field. First, the species should be at least moderately decay-resistant. Second, in cases where detailed profiles are involved, you need a wood that can be sawed well—one that is straight-grained, without knots, and not prone to split. Finally, the wood should not warp when it gets wet and dries. Because your windvane or whirligig will live in a very demanding environment, it's inevitable that it will gain moisture during wet or humid periods and dry at other times. Some woods tolerate this abuse better than others.

With the knowledge that some woodworkers will take exception—choosing wood species can bring on an almost religious zealotry—here are the species we recommend:

First, banak. If you haven't heard of it, don't feel sheltered. It doesn't grow in your backyard—unless you're Brazilian. Banak is a reddish-brown, medium-density wood that is very stable and rot resistant. It saws easily and is very unlikely to split. Paint goes on well—as long as you don't demand an absolutely smooth surface. Banak is open-grained, making it difficult to sand to a mirror-like sheen. About the only other caveat worth mentioning is its origin. And, though it does come from the tropics, most banak is now grown on plantations, so the environmental effect is reduced. In fact, that's the reason banak has become so readily available.

Other good choices that are available in most areas include Douglas fir, redwood, and white oak. But if you've ever shopped for them, you know that they're quite expensive. Besides, clear, straight-grained Douglas fir and redwood come mainly from old-growth forests. We won't get into the environmental issues here, except to say that it might be best to save these woods for applications where there are no good substitutes.

Locally, you may find noncommercial species such as poplar, yew, osage orange, black locust, or others. All work reasonably well and are economical.

Two wood species normally used for demanding applications don't work particularly well for whirligigs and windvanes. Cedar is generally too brittle and stringy to saw in complex curves, and cypress is prone to splinter when sawed or nailed.

MECHANICAL PARTS

Use only corrosion-resistant metal parts in your projects. Screws and nails should be galvanized (either hot-dipped or electro-galvanized) steel, brass, or stainless steel. Just about any hardware store will carry galvanized nails and screws; they'll also have a limited selection of brass fasteners in a compartmented case. Few hardware stores stock stainless wood or machine screws, but they can be ordered through the mail.

Most of the crankshafts in our projects are made from 1/8" brass welding rod. Top quality brazing rod is ideal. It's very corrosion resistant and bends readily. Steel welding rod is better for connecting rods, since they must resist compression and tension. A smaller size (1/16" or 3/32") is fine in all but the most difficult applications.

Some of our designs with particularly complicated crankshafts have tubular bushings to offer additional support. As it happens, 1/8" brass tubing works perfectly with the 1/8" welding rod. You do, however, have to cut and position the bushings on the shafts before bending in the throws.

TOOLS

Whirligigs and windvanes can be built with the simplest of tools. A coping saw (a C-shaped frame with a handle and a thin blade strung across the opening), a drill and bits, and basic handtools are enough to build nearly every project in this book. There is one mandatory handtool that you wouldn't commonly associate with woodworking: locking-jaw pliers. These are essential in bending crank mechanisms, as we'll detail in a little while.

Though handtools are sufficient, it will often be easier to build whirligigs and windvanes if you have a more sophisticated shop. A bandsaw, for example, will save your sawing arm untold agony. It's also a heck of a lot easier to keep the cut square to the surface of the material with a bandsaw than it is with a coping saw. Of course, because the details of the profiles are so fine, you'll need to have a scrolling blade on the bandsaw. There may even be a few of you who have power scroll saws. That tool is a perfect addition to an enthusiastic whirligig builder's shop, offering the ability to saw very tight corners with an amazing degree of control.

A tablesaw is the most likely stationary power tool to find in any shop. And, though it's not required equipment for whirligig construction, it can come in mighty handy. One frequent use of the tablesaw is in ripping the trough for the crankshaft. Because most combination blades leave a 1/8"-wide kerf, you can just set the blade depth to 1/8" and run the stock along the rip fence to form the 1/8" x 1/8" channel for the 1/8" rod.

In a few instances, we used a thickness planer to prepare stock of exactly the thickness we wanted. If you have a planer, by all means use it. In general, though, there are plywoods that can be used in most any circumstance.

It should go without saying that power-tools deserve respect. When working with small pieces of wood, keep your fingers away from moving blades by using push sticks or other aids. Bear in mind, too, that wood dust is good for neither your lungs nor your eyes. Wear an appropriate dust mask when working wood—and even consider wearing a respirator when sawing exotic species with powerful resins, such as walnut and cedar. Safety glasses should be a standard part of your attire.

ASSEMBLY

WORKING WITH THE PATTERNS

If you decide to use the exact profiles we've provided, all you have to do is "loft" the dimensions to suit your materials. The simplest way is just to use the one-square-equals-one-inch approach we've provided. But you could almost as easily make one square equal to 3/4" or 2" to make a smaller or larger project. Just bear in mind that material thicknesses should be adjusted accordingly.

Rather than drawing right on your material, you'll probably want to make a pattern on paper and then trace it onto the stock. Before you start cutting, plan your sawing approaches. Seldom will you be able to start from one side and saw all the way around. More often, you'll have to come in from two directions to make inside corners. Further, it's very difficult to enter the edge of a piece of wood at a very shallow angle; exiting at a shallow angle is much easier.

Even after you've become proficient with the saw, you can expect to do some smoothing of the curves with a file and sandpaper. When filing or sanding plywood, be sure to work toward the center of the material. Otherwise, you'll splinter the outer laminations.

PROPELLERS

These are obviously one of the most crucial parts of a whirligig. The blades themselves are relatively simple to make. Just follow our pattern, adjusting the size or number of blades to suit your project. In general, the more throws there are in a crank, the larger and/or more numerous the blades should be. Most can get by with four blades, but a few—a western windmill, for example—will need six.

However many blades you use, be sure to balance them. You can make a crude scale by balancing a length of welding rod with string tied on each end on the back of a chair. Attach a propeller to each string, and the assembly ought to stay balanced. Use one blade as the standard and adjust all the others to match it.

The trickiest part about propeller making is the hub. The hole for the crankshaft has to be exactly in the middle, and the slots for the blades need to be at equal angles. Here's how we did it.

Start with a square of stock that's as wide as the desired diameter of the hub you're building. Make sure it's *exactly* square. Draw lines on one broad face that connect the opposite corners. These two lines will cross at the exact center. Drill your crankshaft hole here.

With that done, find the point exactly in the middle of an edge (side to side and across the thickness) and use a 45 degree marking bevel to draw a line that passes through this center point. Then move 1/16" to each side of this line and draw new lines. The resulting 1/8"-wide path marks the location of the slot. Repeat this marking procedure for each of the three other sides. Be sure the four slots are all going in the same direction. And be very careful to mark these accurately. Even small errors will produce a noticeable imbalance.

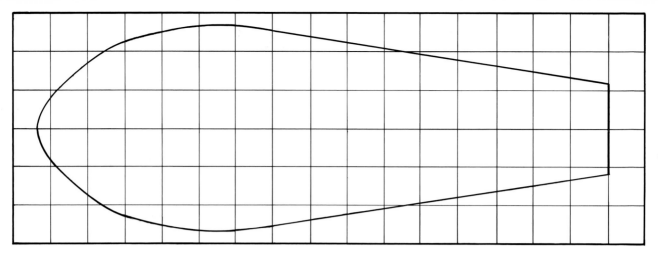

STANDARD 16½" DIAMETER PROPELLER

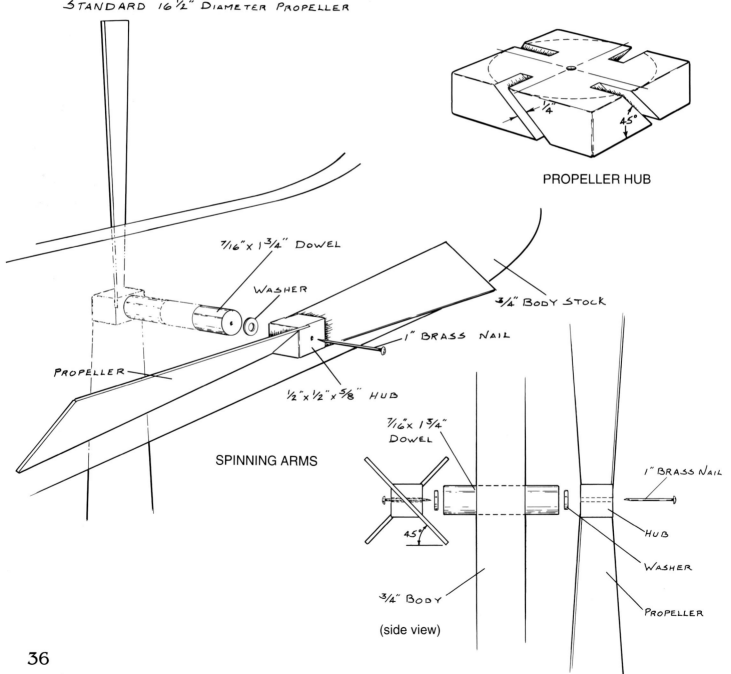

PROPELLER HUB

7/16" × 1¾" DOWEL

WASHER

3/4" BODY STOCK

1" BRASS NAIL

PROPELLER

½" × ½" × 5/8" HUB

SPINNING ARMS

7/16" × 1¾" DOWEL

1" BRASS NAIL

HUB

WASHER

PROPELLER

45°

3/4" BODY

(side view)

CONSTRUCTION TECHNIQUES

Set your miter box or tablesaw miter gauge to 45 degrees, adjust the depth stops or blade height to 1/2" (or other depth, if appropriate) and position the edge so that the blade will run through the marked slot. Cut all four slots and then reduce the square to a round by bandsawing, filing, or a combination of the two.

ADHESIVES

Much of the gluing in whirligigs is unusual for woodworking because it involves bonding face to face rather than edge to edge. Consequently, the demands on glues are somewhat different.

Some glues are easy to apply; some are strong; others are inexpensive; still others are waterproof. None is all four. So we're talking compromise. We're going to recommend the two extremes and let you know about the intermediate options.

If you want to be sure your project hangs together—and don't want to worry too much about fasteners—use epoxy. Sure, it's the most expensive adhesive available; it has to be mixed; and what you don't use goes to waste. But it works.

If you don't want to spend the money or deal with the hassle of epoxy, use plain old carpenter's glue—called yellow or aliphatic resin—and plenty of fasteners. It's not waterproof, but it's cheap. And as long as everything stays tight, and a good coating of paint protects the joints, no water will get to the glue.

In between those two extremes lie resorcinol—the most waterproof and most miserable-to-use glue—and hot melt glue, which is fairly water resistant (the white version) but comparatively weak and ill-suited to gluing boards face to face.

MECHANISMS

Bending accurate throws into crankshafts takes a bit of practice. The difficulty isn't so much in making the bends as it is in making four of them precisely enough to form a U and return to the same axis. The technique we finally settled on employs locking-jaw pliers. Clamp the rod in the jaws so it's perpendicular to the handles, and make the first 90 degree bend. Then open the pliers, move them exactly one jaw width along the rod, and form the next 90 degree corner. Repeat this process to form the completed crank. To form cranks with different depths of stroke, different size locking-jaw pliers can be used (they come in a variety of sizes and jaw configurations). While the depth of stroke may vary, the lateral bend at the bottom should remain about 3/4" so that the push rod connection doesn't wander and jam. We suggest either of two methods for connecting push rods. The easier way is to coil the rod 3 or 4 turns around the crank. If you have a welding torch, you may want to weld washers on either side of the rod connection.

To attach propellers and other hardware, one end of the crank is threaded. You'll need a no.6 x 32 (no. 6 is the diameter and 32 is the number of threads per inch) die and wrench. If you're not familiar with these tools, just ask your hardware store. You should be able to get what you need for between $5 and $10. Making threads is surprisingly easy. The only trick is to proceed in half-revolution increments, backing off to clear metal chips from the teeth of the die. Otherwise, the threads will be poorly formed, or, worse, the rod or die may break.

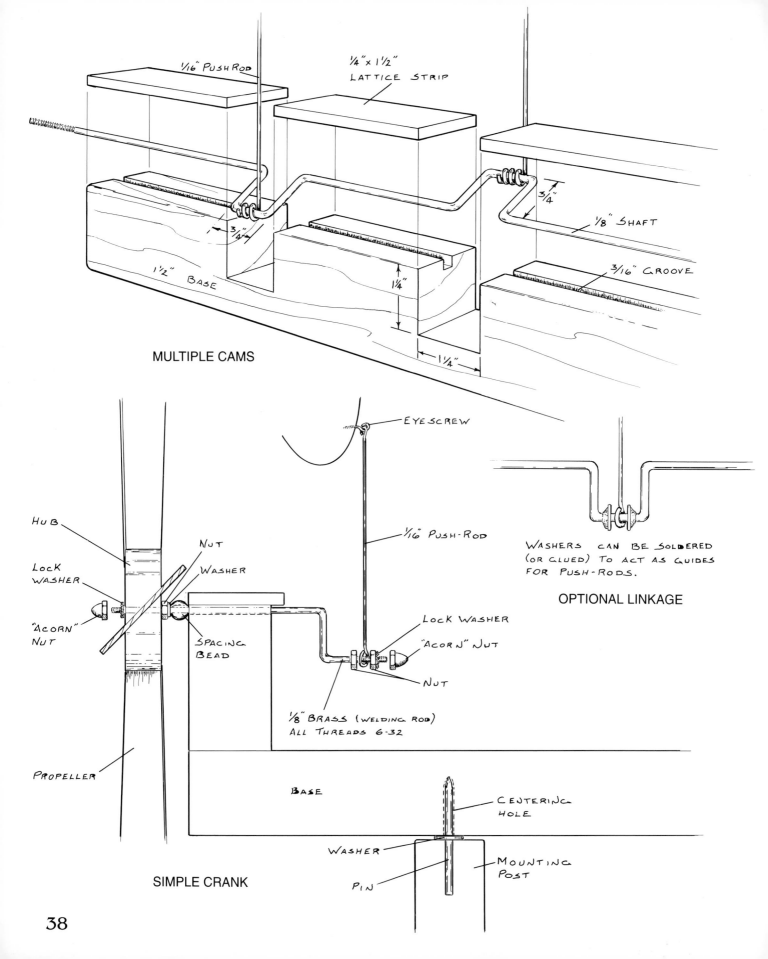

1/16" PUSH ROD

1/4" × 1 1/2" LATTICE STRIP

3/4"

1/8" SHAFT

3/16" GROOVE

3/4"

1 1/2" BASE

1 1/4"

1 1/4"

MULTIPLE CAMS

EYESCREW

1/16" PUSH-ROD

HUB

LOCK WASHER

"ACORN" NUT

NUT

WASHER

SPACING BEAD

LOCK WASHER

"ACORN" NUT

NUT

PROPELLER

1/8" BRASS (WELDING ROD) ALL THREADS 6-32

BASE

CENTERING HOLE

WASHER

PIN

MOUNTING POST

SIMPLE CRANK

WASHERS CAN BE SOLDERED (OR GLUED) TO ACT AS GUIDES FOR PUSH-RODS.

OPTIONAL LINKAGE

FINISHES

Creative painting is at least as important to the successful whirligig or windvane as is woodworking. And many of our projects have been painted by craftspeople who rightly deserve the title artist. Don't be intimidated, though. It's not all that hard to get the hang of shading and blending.

The basic principle of blending paints is to apply the predominant color first as a base coat. Then put a small amount of the base coat and a small amount of the paint you want to blend onto separate areas of your pallet (a small piece of wood). Dip the brush in the base coat and then stick one corner into the shade paint. Work the brush on a clean part of the pallet until the edge between the two colors blends suitably. Then apply the paint to your work.

Although enamels can be used, most of our projects were painted with acrylics (available at craft and art supply stores). You can buy these in small tubes, which will allow you to use several different colors without investing a fortune in paint. Because the acrylic isn't weather resistant, we applied two coats of sunlight-resistant polyurethane varnish once the acrylic was thoroughly cured. This also seals glue joints and other exposed surfaces from the relentless weathering out-of-doors.

SITING

If your whirligig or windvane is going to be more than a conversation piece, you want to mount it where it's windy. The perfect spot, of course, is a rooftop. Wind speed drops dramatically closer to the ground, and it also becomes turbulent, making a wind toy gyrate alarmingly. Unless your project is very large, though, you'll probably want to have it a little closer to admiring eyes.

To find a conducive spot in your yard, you first need to know which direction the prevailing wind comes from. In most areas, this will vary with the seasons. During winter, it will come from the west or northwest, and as the weather warms, it will shift to the southwest or south. (There are significant local exceptions to this general trend. Local effects may be much more important than general trends in mountainous areas or near the sea.)

Once you've determined the prevailing wind direction, look for a spot that's well upwind from buildings or trees. If the only clear site available is downwind from obstructions, move a distance downwind equal to three times the height of any such obstruction. Even here, it will help if you can mount your whirligig or windvane at least eight feet above the ground.

As for mounting, we prefer a simple 1/4" steel pin driven into a 3/16" hole drilled in the end of a pressure-treated 4 x 4. Drill a 1/4" hole in the wind toy and apply a little soap to the pin to help the wood pivot easily on it. Place a fender washer between the top of the post and the underside of the project to reduce friction. Remember that the pivot point needs to be in front of the centerline of the whirligig or windvane, so that the aft section will act as a tail.

If you end up feeling so proud of your project that you want to keep it inside where you can admire it, less stout mounting will work fine. Substitute a short 2 x 2 for the 4 x 4 and a smaller rod if you like. After all, a window fan shouldn't develop any threatening gusts.

MEDICINE MAN

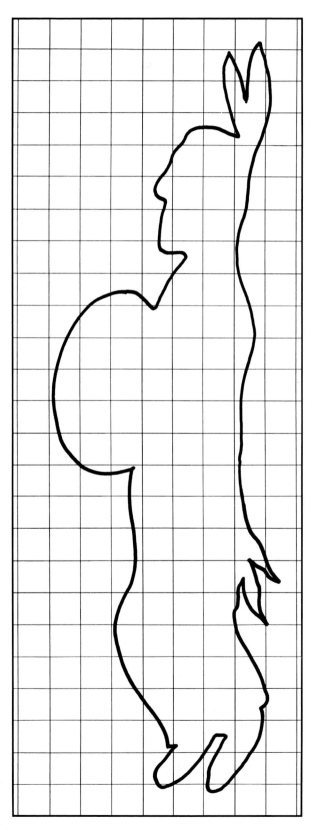

Good medicine in any weather, this stylized native American shaman is modeled after a traditional windvane design, akin to the "Hex Doctor" motif that North America's European settlers believed guarded their dwellings against curses. Interestingly enough, the whites of that period considered theirs the more sophisticated culture.

As with most of the windvanes in this collection, there's very little we can offer in terms of construction tips. If made to scale, the windvane would probably be best built out of 1/2" or 3/4" solid stock or plywood. However, the design doesn't include too many intricate cuts, and could be built to most any scale.

Painting, as usual, is pretty much up to you, though you may use our example as a guide. We do suggest that you include a sash—made of thin strips of nylon, yarn, etc.—and trim it with brightly colored feathers to provide additional movement and excitement as the vane turns in the wind.

Note the somewhat unique mounting; this windvane "stands up", avoiding the more traditional horizontal mount. Drill a 1/4" hole into the bottom of the drum as shown, and mount the weathervane on a soaped 1/4" steel pin driven into a 3/16" diameter hole in a pressure-treated post.

This "medicine man" may not serve to keep hexes away, but he might well serve as a reminder that we should never judge another until we've walked a mile in his moccasins.

MERMAID

A Fish Named Wanda? When first the schooner Hesperus sailed the wintry sea, it's likely that her bowsprit was graced with a finny femme fatale similar to Wanda here. Such carvings were believed to serve as charms against storms, and their ever-forward gaze would, it was hoped, lead the ship home after its wanderings. Well, a number of those wooden hulks failed to return, so we have to doubt the protective abilities of these seagoing amulets. It's a safe bet, though, that Wanda and her sisters had profound impact upon the imaginations of many ship-

loads of romance-hungry seamen. What else but long months of mentally "playing the scales" could cause otherwise reliable men to mistake the homely, walrus-like manitee for a mermaid?

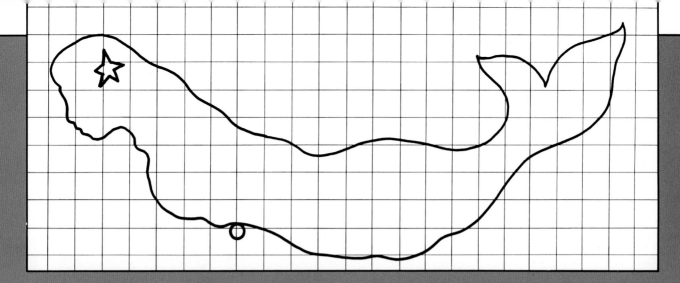

The basic figure should be cut, using our grid pattern as a guide, from either 3/4" lumber or 1/2" marine plywood. You may want to re-scale the pattern to suit your materials or site.

The starfish barrettes that adorn Wanda's locks should be cut from 1/4" plywood. A greater feeling of depth can be achieved by cutting the mermaid's arms from 1/4" plywood and affixing them, also. Then drill the pivot hole in her belly.

To paint the mermaid, we chose fairly traditional colors, gobbing on the paint when making the pearl necklace for a high relief effect. You can, of course, use as much detail as patience allows when marking the scales on Wanda's nether parts. We used a metallic paint, but you might go so far as to glue on sequins for the ultimate in girlish glitter.

Add a plastic or wooden macramé bead as a bearing on your post pin, and let your salty siren sing her seductive song into the face of the wind.

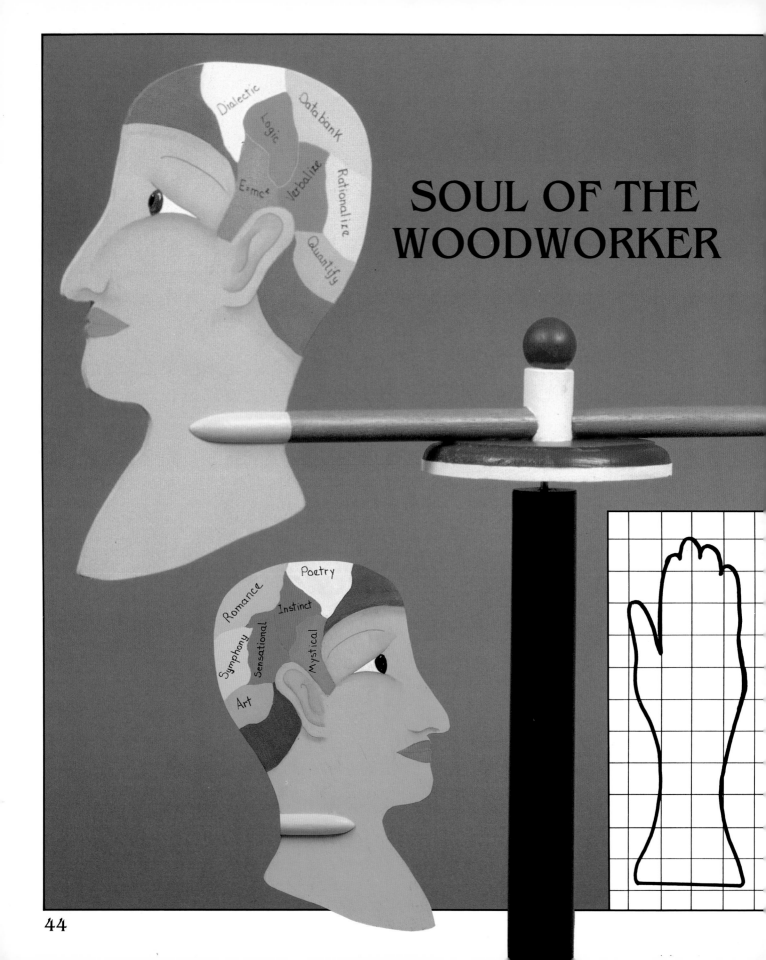

SOUL OF THE WOODWORKER

This traditional design is usually referred to as "head and hand"—too prosaic a label for a windvane that symbolizes the central theme of this collection: fine handicrafts are created when nimble hands are driven by playful minds. In fact, the point where dexterity and imagination meet—in the case of this windmill, its pivot point—is where you're most likely to find a woodworker's soul.

The base (connecting the head and hand) is a 22" length of 3/4" dowel. Use your tablesaw to cut 1/4"-wide (double kerf) slots to a depth of 2" from each end, then sand the slotted ends to an eye-pleasing taper.

The head and hand can follow our grid pattern, or you can create your own patterns (consider personalizing the windvane by tracing the shadowed profile of a friend!).

Reach Out and Touch ...

To form the axle, drill a 3/4" hole through a 2" length of 1-1/4" dowel (closet rod), and glue the base dowel inside this hole. Cut a 5" disk to form the base for the axle dowel, which is glued on top of its center. The assembly can be completed by a decorative bead, cabinet knob, or any similar piece of wooden trim.

Drill the mounting hole in the base, then go on to paint the pivot and rod assembly, the head, and the hand before assembling the windvane. You'll notice that we differentiated between the right and left sides of the brain in our labeling. Feel free to follow our example, or use your own imagination to determine what your windvane will have on its mind.

LEONARDO'S HELICOPTER

Leonardo da Vinci—the 15th-Century painter, anatomist, engineer, and inventor who was the bastard son of Ser Piero of Vinci, Italy—is in many ways the patriarch of the whirligig. His studies of the dynamics of air currents are the first recorded rational exploration of the potential for human flight. And the helicopter that resulted—though probably never more than sketches in his notebooks—really works. Leonardo looked deeply to understand what made things work.

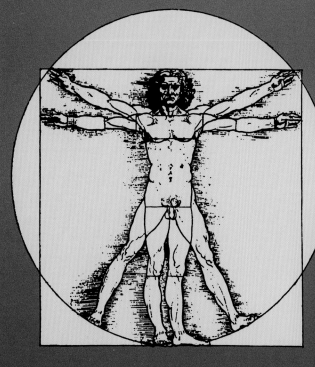

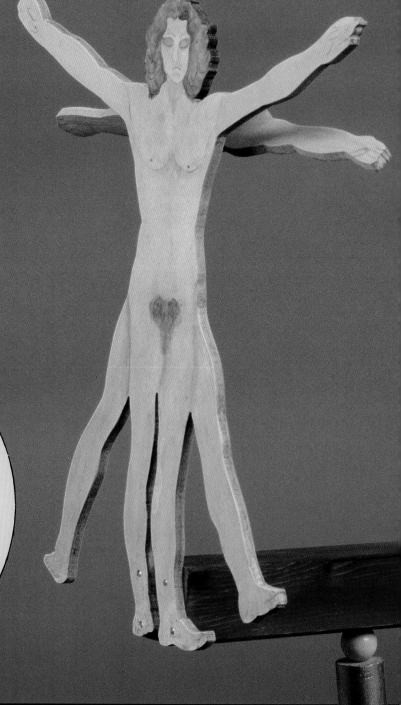

Leonardo probably envisioned his helicopter as an inclined plane—a screw biting into the wind to rise vertically. But he was likely also aware that a breeze perpendicular to the device's axis would set it spinning—an effect of no small significance. Mechanisms that translate motion through a right angle are the foundation of all technology.

Our rendition of the inventor's aircraft uses a few materials that might have been a revelation to him. The shaft—a wooden target arrow—would have been familiar enough, though its forged steel point resting in the hole in the base would probably have drawn comment. The spool that serves as the main bushing would almost certainly have been a curiosity. And the plywood disks that make up the upper and lower supports might have sent him into paroxysms of delight and wonderment. Once we'd explained refrigeration, we expect he would have been

keenly interested in the popsicle sticks that fan from the axle to form the wing. (Tongue depressors work even better below.) We'd like to think that he would have approved of the holes we bored in those wooden paddles to slide them over the shaft. But it's a lot more fun to imagine his reaction to the device we drilled them with.

Out front stands our rendition of Leonardo's archetypal man. This is probably not a self-portrait. The artist did do them, but this drawing was a part of his anatomy notebooks—rigor-

ously scientific renditions based on his dissection of more than 30 corpses. Our figure's arms (actually propeller blades in a hub) spin, demonstrating, as Leonardo's illustrations did, the patterns and range of motion of the human body.

Leonardo fascinates not only for the quality of his work but also for the nature of it. He embodies a time when there was no distinction between science and art. And that's as good a frame of mind for whirligig building as we can imagine.

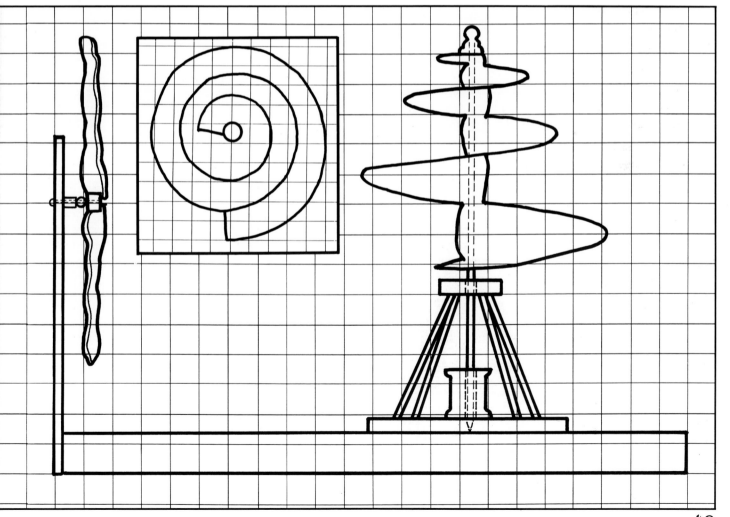

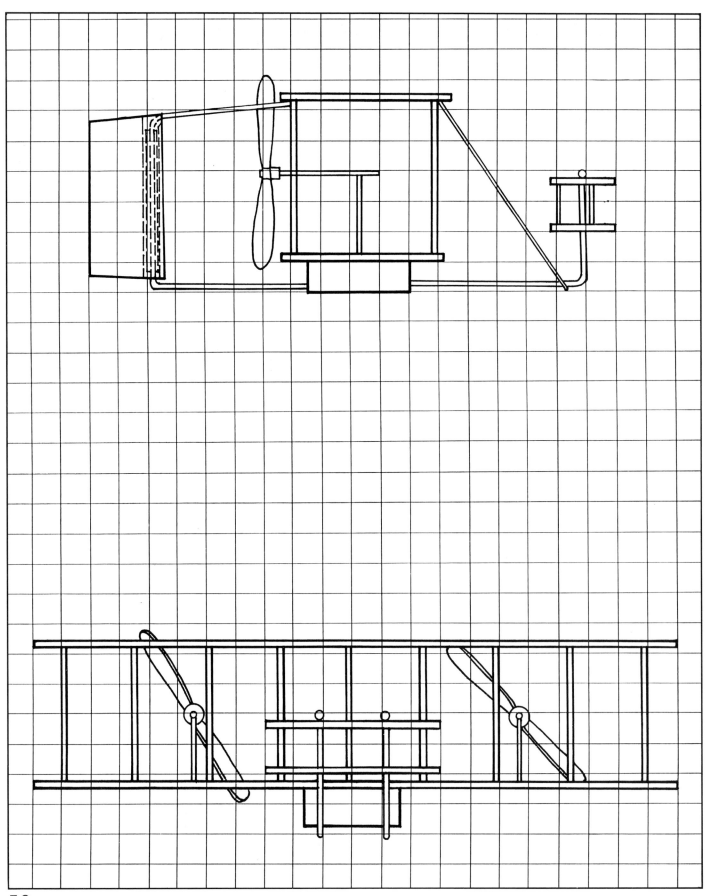

WRIGHT MADE RIGHT

Just what is the difference between a whirligig and an airplane? Is it only a matter of scale that separates tool from toy? Unlike many of the projects in this book, this is no caricature. It's an accurate scale model of the Wright brothers' Kitty Hawk conveyance. Even the rudder is functional. But this one's wind-powered.

Rather than try to detail the construction of this project step by step, we're going to outline techniques to lead you in the Wright direction.

All air foils are formed from 1/4" plywood. The vertical struts that separate the wings are 1/4" dowels. All the support struts—even those in the front canard—are triangulated with 22-gauge brass wire. To simplify threading, we drilled small holes near the top and bottom of each dowel-strut before installing them. This makes weaving the fine strands that draw the wing structure into compression relatively easy.

The front canard and the tail assembly are attached to the 2 x 4 block below the wings with 1/8" brazing rod—with a number of soldered-on attachments. To allow threading into the 2 x 4, brass screws are soldered in place. In front, washers support the base of the front pod, with sections of 1/8" brass tube slid over the rods to separate the upper and lower surfaces. Then the end of the rods are threaded and brass cap screws snugged down.

In back, the pair of brazing rod supports converge to form a pivot for the tail assembly. The two parallel tail panels are attached to a brass tube that slides over the pivot-rod.

The two vertical propeller supports are 1/8" brazing rod, threaded so that a standard brass nut goes on top of the lower wing and a cap nut goes below. Atop these two rods, a 1/8" brass tube serves as the bushing for the propeller shaft. It has to be soldered to the vertical supports (off the model), keeping the heat as low as possible to avoid warping the tube. The propellers spin on more 1/8" brazing rod, threaded on both ends, with nuts to lock everything down, yet allowing the props to spin freely.

The propellers themselves are made by the same method as the larger ones used in other projects—except that they have only two blades each and measure 6-1/2" in diameter. It's mighty fine work, but that's what this project is all about.

THE ADDLED
PLANETARIUM

THE ADDLED PLANETARIUM

With all due respect to professor Adler, creating an astronomically correct model of our solar system just isn't conducive to craft. With Mars the size of a small marble and Jupiter as large as a basketball, how would you balance the weights of the various planets to rotate around a sun the size of a Volkswagen Beetle? With that in mind, we're sure you'll be glad we've taken certain scientific liberties.

The secret of this project is balance. Each of the two "propellers," composed of opposing planets that are balanced, spins separately. We kept the planets roughly the same size so we wouldn't have to vary their distances from the axle too much to compensate. However, you could use different thicknesses of material that would allow different diameter planets without changing weights. But we chose the simpler option of using 1/2" throughout.

To balance each pair of planets, attach them to the 3/8" dowel *before* you drill the axle hole in the dowel. Use 3/16" two-ended woodscrews set into the dowel ends for mounting. (These will let you adjust the planet's angle to catch the wind.) Then balance each assembly on a sharp edge to figure out exactly where to drill the axle hole.

The planets can be cut out with hole saws and/or a scroll saw, as is the case with Saturn and the flares of the sun.

The shooting star is cut from a single piece of 1/2" plywood. We raised the star's edges a little with a bead of glue, which accentuates the glittery paint.

The propeller-axle arrangement deserves a little explanation. On this project, you'll need 1/8" (or larger) steel welding rod for extra strength. The sun is fixed on the end of the axle with a cap nut. The two planet-dowels are separated on the axle by a section of brass tube and washers slid over the axle. Wooden beads separate the planet dowel from the shooting star, into which a threaded end of the axle is screwed, leaving just enough room for the assemblies to spin freely.

As for paint, it's clear why we picked the planets we did. Saturn's rings are, of course, spectacular. Jupiter's red spot and pearlish blue-green are equally amazing. But when it comes to sheer beauty, there's no place like home.

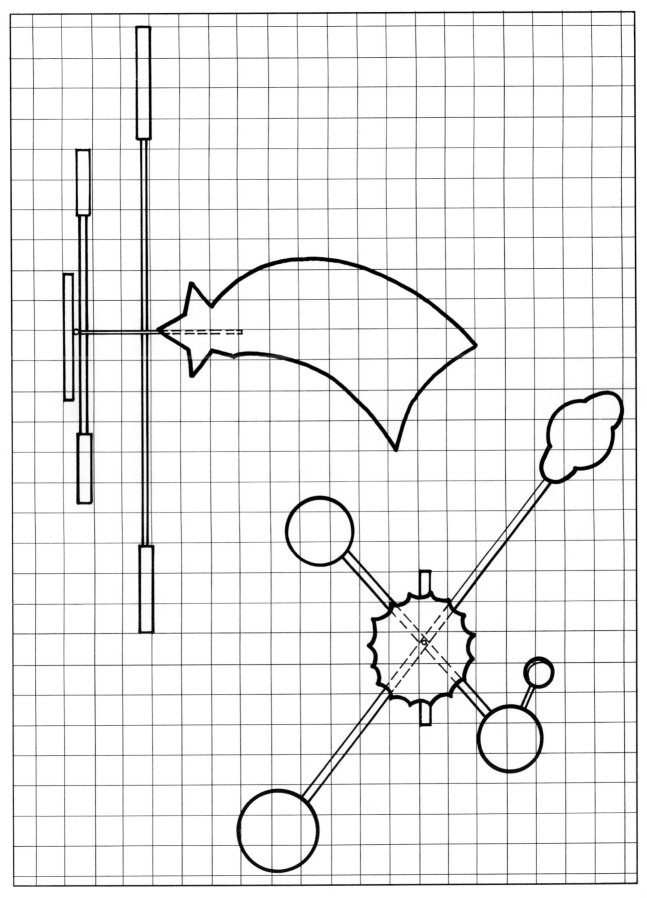

HOT PURSUIT

It's a rivalry on the scale of light vs. darkness, good vs. evil, or even Coke vs. Pepsi. Yes, the deserts of the Southwest must be crisscrossed by now with the endless trails of smugly fleeing roadrunners and ever-optimistic coyotes...not to mention the smoking remains of various rocket skates, giant slingshots, and other implements of destruction !

HOT PURSUIT

This is probably as simple in concept as any whirligig in our collection. Its design lends itself to any variation on the pursuit theme, with one character's arms and the other's legs spinning vigorously. Instead of wildfowl and predatory canine, you might opt for cop and robber, cat and mouse, truant officer and delinquent, or investor and Savings & Loan officer!

The base of the whirligig can be as big as you need to accommodate the figures (do make sure, though, that there's room for both "propellers" to swing at the same time!). Cut the base from any 1 or 2x stock. The coyote, roadrunner, and the distant, scenic mesa are fashioned from 1/2" stock.

The spinning arms and legs are, as you can see in the photograph, really nothing more than two-bladed propellers. In fact, we'd recommend that you make them more propeller-shaped than those you see. Painting the limbs upon the oversized blades will leave more surface to catch the wind and assure better spin in questionable breezes.

You might want to tack nails into the base, after marking where the figures will go; then cut off their heads at a height of about 1/4" using wire cutters. You can drill matching holes in the bases of the figures and glue them down. Before doing that, though, drive appropriate brads through the holes in the propeller hubs and into the figures behind. You want them tight enough to prevent excessive wobble but loose enough to let the arms and legs spin freely. With all the pieces cut to shape and sanded, you can go ahead and paint the players to suit your fancy.

There may be a lesson for all of us in this whirligig. The poor old coyote never gets any closer...but he never *gives up*, either!

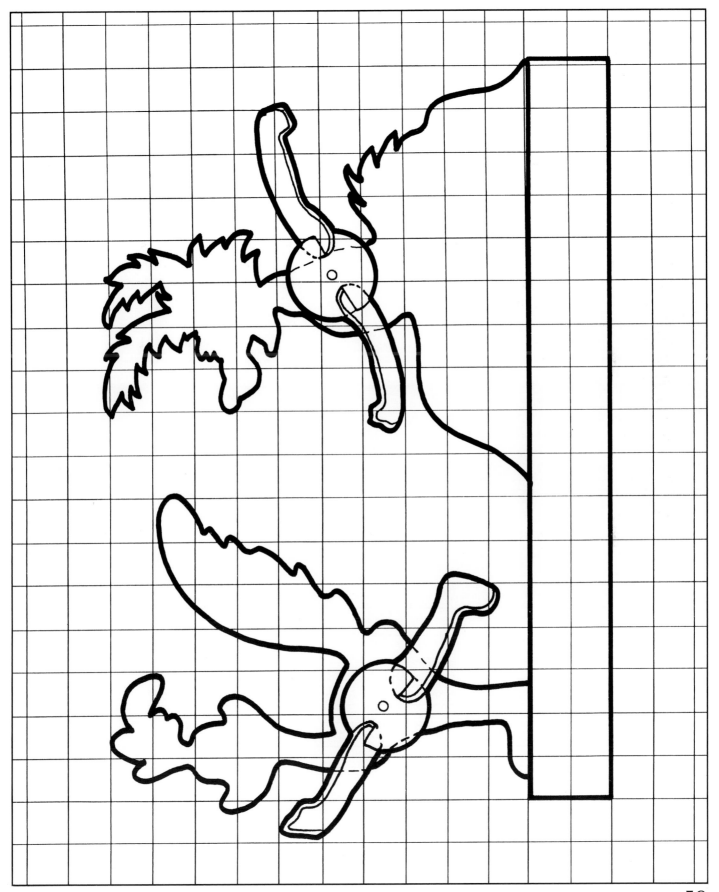

VIKING SHIP

Scholars are pretty much
agreed now that several centuries
before Columbus inadvertently
bumped into San Salvador, Vikings had
explored much of the northeastern coast
of the New World, and may even have established colonies. Though much less is known
about these early Scandinavian vessels than
the Nina, Pinta, and Santa Maria, our design
is authentically based on old wood carvings.
And so in the tradition of maritime weathervanes, this whirligig pays homage
to the earliest known seafaring
explorers of America.

VIKING SHIP

The Viking ship's hull can be made of any 3/4"-thick straight-grained wood that saws well across and with the grain. We used mahogany, but fir would also work well. The sail consists of one big piece of 1/4" plywood that extends all the way out to the shrouds and down to the deck. It's the paint that creates the deception of detail in the photograph.

We used chisels to form a 1/4" groove in the deck to receive the sail. But if you're not up to that sort of labor, you could simply tack 1/4" braces on each side of the sail at its junction to the hull. The 3/16" dowel boom and 5/16" dowel mast are simply glued to the top of the sail.

The only tricky part of the construction is making the spinning oars. It's not that they're all that complicated, they're just small and numerous. The oars themselves are pieces of tongue depressor filed slightly to improve their aerodynamics. They're notched into 1/2" hubs of solid stock (mahogany in our case). To enhance the amount of gluing area for oar to hub, we left the hubs square. The axle for these propellers is simply a nail that's a loose fit in a hole drilled through the hub. We suggest using a small handsaw to cut the angled notches for the blades—a backed miter saw in a miter box is ideal. Be sure to position the oars far enough apart to clear each other when spinning.

This is another case where paint makes the project. The detail of the dragon and the sail can go any way you like, though we'd suggest that there's little precedent for any elaborate rigging. Oh, and don't forget the bright streamer atop the mast. The Vikings' austere nature may not have inclined them towards ensigns, but a rich oral heritage suggests they would have appreciated a "tell-tale."

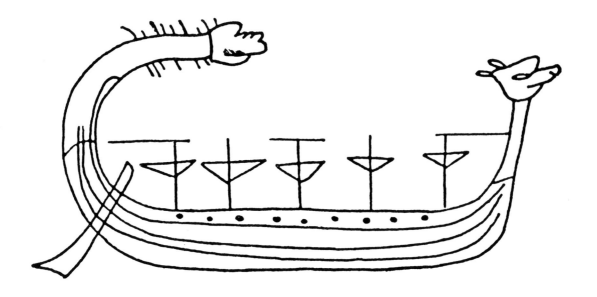

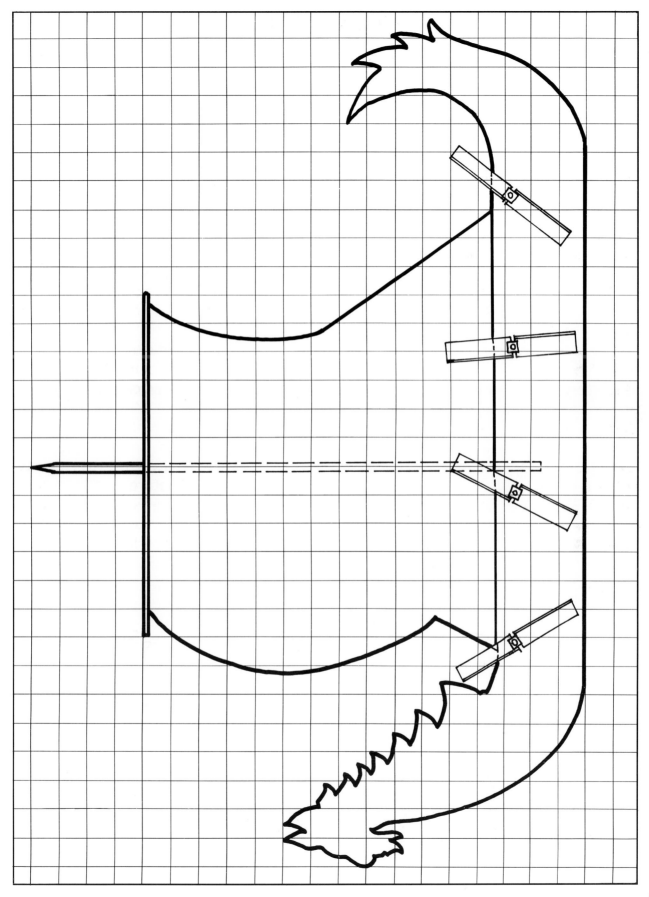

THE HUMMER OF SUMMER

Tiny hummingbirds are among the most beautiful of nature's baubles, and among the most ethereal. They hover, trembling at the mouth of a flower, and then—before you can fetch an appreciative friend to enjoy the visitation—the magical birds are gone. Our hummingbird, on the other hand, is a "bird in the hand." If your skills are up to the task, he can be almost as beautiful as his wild brethren, but he'll be happy to stay around and perform for you as long as the breezes blow.

THE HUMMER OF SUMMER

Though a fairly simple whirligig, this sipping hummingbird has an appealing balance—the throbbing of the propeller effectively countering the more frantic hovering of the bird. Its charm belies the lack of headaches in its construction.

Our base is a 2 x 2-1/2" x 14-1/2" piece of banak, with a 1/4"-thick strip ripped from one of the 2" x 14-1/2" sides. Now, take the remaining base piece and, with a tablesaw (preferably) or a handsaw cut a 1/8"-deep by 1/8"-wide saw kerf, centered, down one of the 2" x 14-1/2" surfaces. The kerf of a tablesaw will be just right; a handsaw kerf may call for a little sanding, filing or hogging out before its trough accepts the 1/8" welding rod crank, letting it spin freely.

The crank itself begins as an 18" length of 1/8" welding rod. Center it in the kerf to determine position, then mark the point to bend the crankshaft to 90°. Measure one inch down that bend, and form the final 90° bend to complete the crank. At this point you can lubricate (with soap or wax) the crank kerf and then glue the 1/4"-thick ripped strip of banak in place over the groove. The rest of the mechanical assembly can wait until the whirligig is completed and painted.

The propeller is 16-1/2" in diameter and follows the basic design detailed in the chapter on construction techniques.

The hummingbird and garden are fashioned from plywood . (We used 3/4" stock, but 1/2" would have been suitable, and the bird could have been formed from 1/4" marine plywood.) As usual, either use our grid line-for-line, or take your inspiration from it and design a bird and bush of your own. In painting, too, feel free to follow our lead or turn to *Petersen's Field Guide to the Birds* for the real thing.

Glue the garden cutout atop the base, lining its front edge with a mark drawn down the center of the base. Now thread both ends of the crankshaft, and slip the shaft through its slot, keeping the crank toward the rear, and secure the propeller with two brass nuts and a brass cap nut.

Mark the position for the hummingbird's pivot points, drill slightly oversized holes, and then drive a wire-brad axle through the upper pivot and into the garden board behind the bird. A length of 1/16" brass rod, cut to fit, is then secured through the bird's lower pivot and wrapped around the crank, where it's held by a pair of brass nuts.

Now just find a spot with a steady breeze, within easy view of a comfortable chair, and settle back to enjoy a little piece of summer, no matter what season it is!

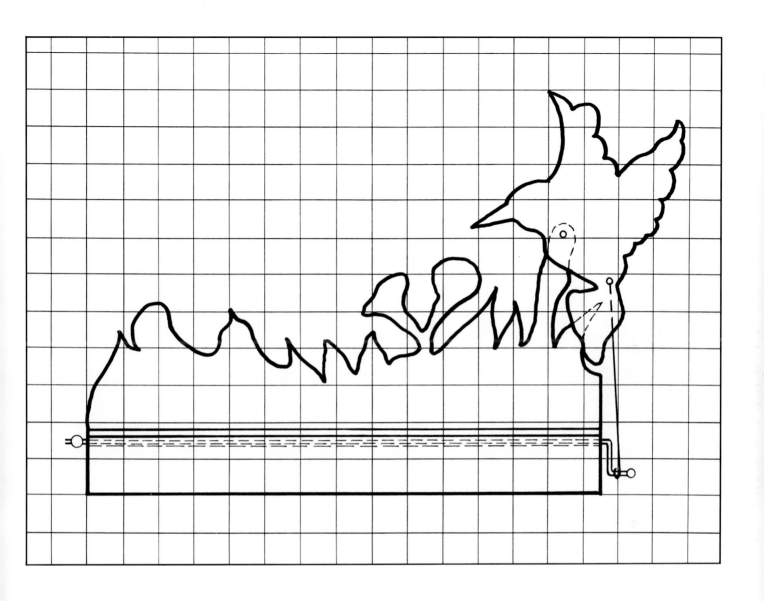

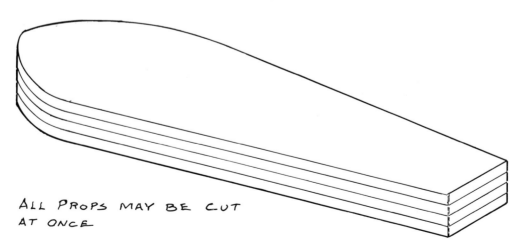

ALL PROPS MAY BE CUT
AT ONCE

HOW THE WEST WAS LOST

What we've got here is a cavalcade of all-but-extinct species. Of these icons of western expansion and resistance—the steam locomotive, the windmill, and the buffalo—none has survived as more than a curiosity. But we'll leave final interpretation of that irony to you. Like the buffalo, you might butt heads with our notions, even if we were only pulling your leg.

HOW THE WEST WAS LOST

The base of our wild-west show is a simple section of 1 x 1-1/2" pine, and all the figures are made from 1/2" plywood. In fact, from a woodworker's standpoint, it's only the propeller that presents new challenges.

To better simulate an old water pump, we decided that six blades was really a minimum. To make the hexagonal hub, take a piece of 1x stock (or thinner, if you've got it), and saw it to form a 1" x 1-5/32" rectangle. Now find the points half way across each 1" face and make a mark. Next, move in 5/32" from each corner along the longer faces, and make marks at those spots. When you connect the marks, you'll have a hexagon. Saw along the lines and cut it out.

To locate the center of the hexagon for the 1/8" axle hole, connect three points. If your cuts were accurate, they all should cross at one point. Miss a little? No problem, just place your axle hole in the center formed by the three lines.

With your tiny hexagon prepared, find the midpoint in each face, and follow the same procedure for propeller slot cutting we described in the chapter on construction techniques. You'll end up with six grooves in the right locations.

As if that wasn't enough, we added another wrinkle of authenticity by engaging each blade in a supporting 5"-diameter ring. Your best bet is to cut the ring out with a coping or saber saw. To install it, we suggest attaching all the blades to the hub first, then notch each one to receive the ring.

The crankshaft on the windmill has about a 1/2" offset for its throw. It connects to the buffalo's heel through a length of 1/16" brass rod. (That's a sucker rod in windmill parlance.) To allow him to rock, the buffalo's forward-most hoof is pierced by one double-nutted end of a brass U-shaped rod, the other end of which fits into a tight hole in the side of the base.

The locomotive and windmill are held to the base with glue and the assistance of nails or screws. There may be some significance to the fact that only the bison moves. Or maybe we've just been buffaloed.

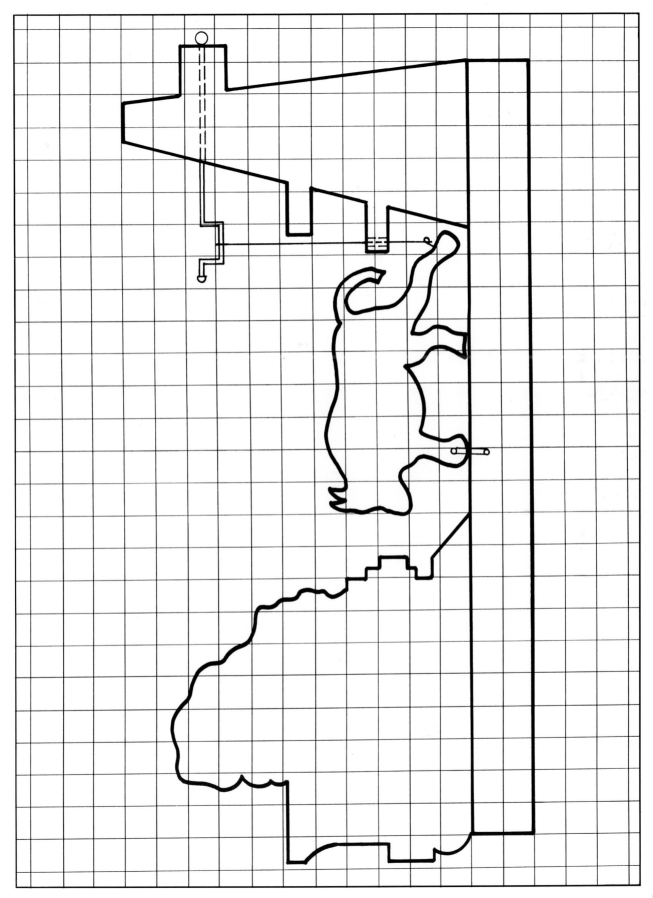

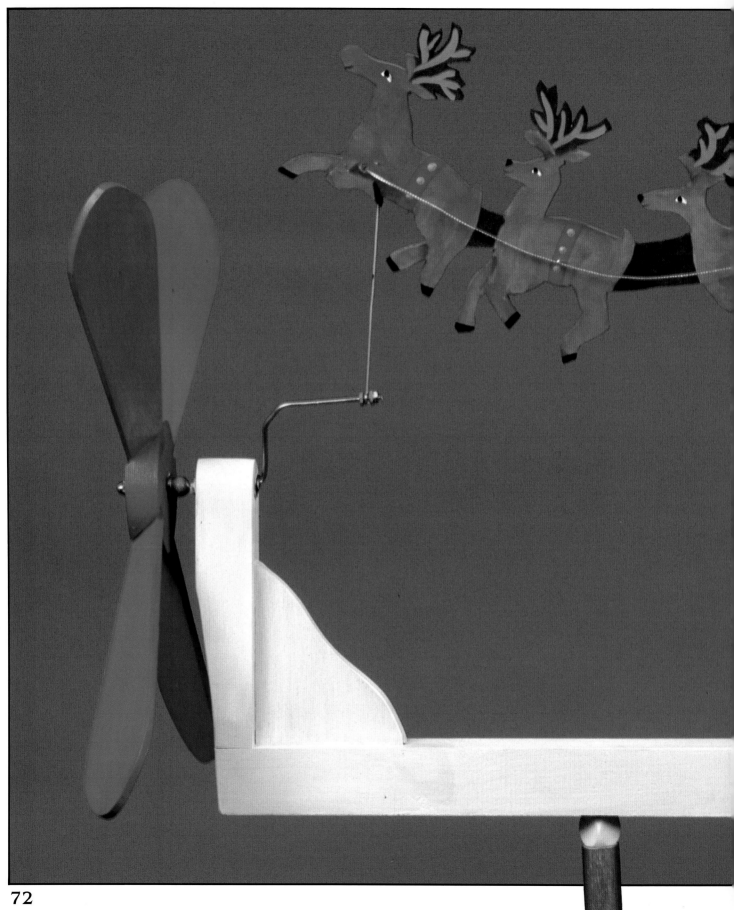

A RIGHT JOLLY OLD ELF

Christmas comes but once a year, but we can get ready for as many months as we'd like. And you might find, as we have, that simply spinning the propeller on this whirligig and making the antlered team leap into the air can invite the holidays into your workshop, well in anticipation of the season of gift-giving.

A RIGHT JOLLY OLD ELF

Here's another design that's far more dramatic in appearance than it is complicated in construction. In fact, it's simple enough to craft that, should you start early, you might end up cranking out a few extras for those on your Christmas list.

As you can see, this attractive whirligig requires a relatively long 1x base. The propeller mounts on an upright at the front of the base, also cut from 1x stock. As you can see in the photograph, we relieved the lower front edge of this upright to allow for the movement of the prop.

The house and moon (which can be cut as a unit or separately to provide a more three-dimensional effect) and the "snowdrift" (that decorates and supports the propeller mount) can all be cut from 1/2" marine plywood. You might well want to exercise a little artistic individuality in the design of the house, perhaps making it duplicate the roofing and door/window arrangement of your own home.

All of this cutting-to-form warrants a bandsaw with a scrolling blade. (Or, better still, a power scroll saw.) In fact, if you don't have one of the two, we'd suggest you make an attempt to borrow one rather than attempt to cope with a coping saw.

As you can see, we've only included four of the "eight tiny reindeer." A stickler for mythic accuracy could cut them out individually and fashion another four to mount on the far side of the reins.

The drive shaft—as usual a length of 1/8" welding rod—runs through an appropriately-sized hole in the upright support. Thread both ends of the rod with the No. 6-32 die before running it through the hole (remember to wax or soap the rod first), bending the longer-than-usual crank, and installing the 16-1/2" diameter propeller with bead spacers and brass nuts.

Painting will be fairly straightforward. You'll probably want to make the base, upright, and snowdrift white. The moon would look silly in anything too far from yellow, and we all know what color Santa's wardrobe is. We chose festive red propeller blades to complete the seasonal motif, although a candycane red-and-white might also be interesting.

A wire brad axle, run through a hole drilled in the sled runner and into the moon, provides a pivot for the reindeer and sleigh, while a length of 1/16" brass rod connects Rudolph to the crankshaft.

And they'll rise from the roof like the down off a thistle.

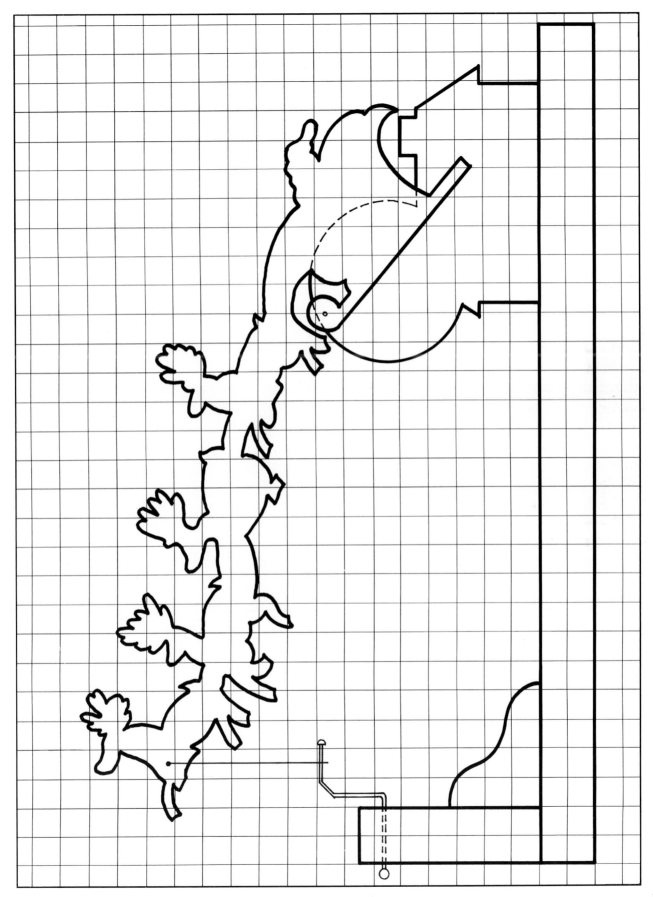

ELVIS'S PELVIS

He's the king, all right. Say anything different in some neighborhoods and you risk violence. Years after his demise, this American icon still vies with "Bigfoot" for tabloid headlines and has inspired armies of sequined, swivel-hipped impersonators. Sure, *reasonable* minds know that the king is dead...but don't you sometimes wonder, maybe just a little?

As impressive as Elvis will look when the propeller is spinning and he's "all shook up", this whirligig is as simple as a crankshaft wind toy can be.

The base is cut from 1x stock. In this case, however, you needn't worry about cutting notches or ripping slats to cover the drive-shaft channel. You can, as we did, cut 1/2" wide by 1/2" deep notches on the ends of the upper surface of the base to allow for secure mounting of the tail (which proudly proclaims the star of our show) and the front support (which can either be glued to, or made part of, the upper body of the figure.)

As you'll deduce from the above, the tail, front support, and upper body of the Elvis figure are all cut from 1/2" marine plywood. (These can be fastened to the base, with glue and perhaps some wire brads.) The hips (that very pelvis that rocked the staid Ed Sullivan show into sudden notoriety) and legs should be cut from 1/4" ply-wood. The propeller for this whirligig is our standard 16-1/2" diameter, four-blade prop, which should provide plenty of driving force to keep "a whole lotta shakin' goin' on."

The actual painting (and even the shaping and cutting) of Elvis allows a lot of room for creative expression. You may choose to portray the king in his early years, still looking lean and mean. You might also decide to portray the more, uh, *substantial* Elvis of the last, tragic days. Regardless, feel free to resort to sequins, glitter paint, stainless-steel studs and the like, when dressing up the monarch of rock'n'roll.

As you can see, the 1/8"-diameter drive shaft simply runs through a 1/8" hole bored through the upright support. Cut the rod to its approximate length, and thread the propeller end with a No. 6-32 die. Then soap the metal, slide it through, and bend the two right angles that form the crank. With that done, you can install the propeller, using brass nuts and bead bearings.

Next, drill the holes in the thighs, pelvis and knees that will keep everything shakin'. Assemble Elvis with small wire-brad pivots; then run a length of 1/16" brass rod between the crankshaft and his leg, and he'll be ready to rock! To wind him up, just find the balance point in the base and bore it to accept the 1/4" diameter steel pin that's already been secured in a post installed...well, why not in front of your own personal heartbreak hotel!

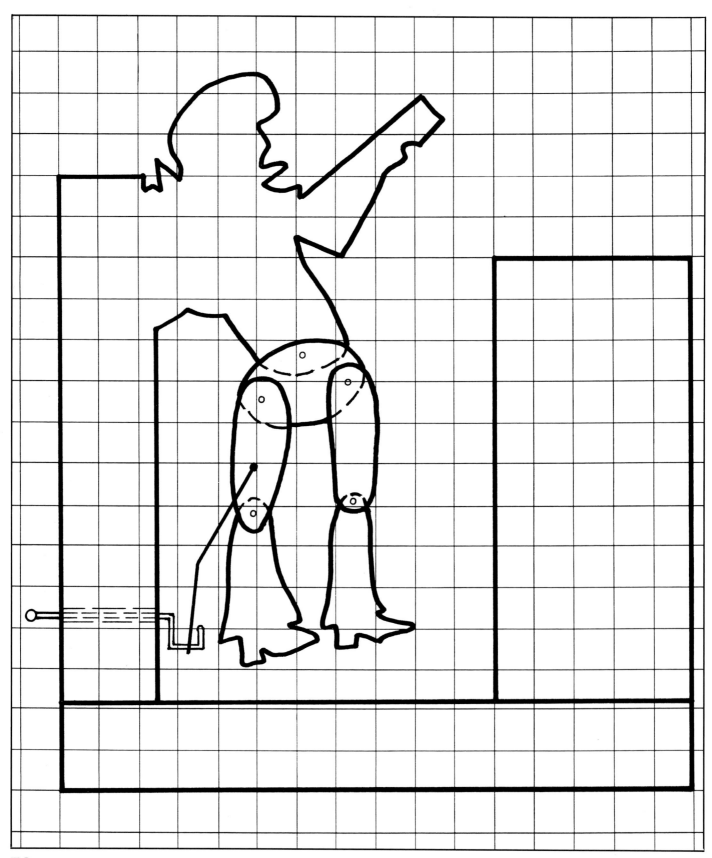

78

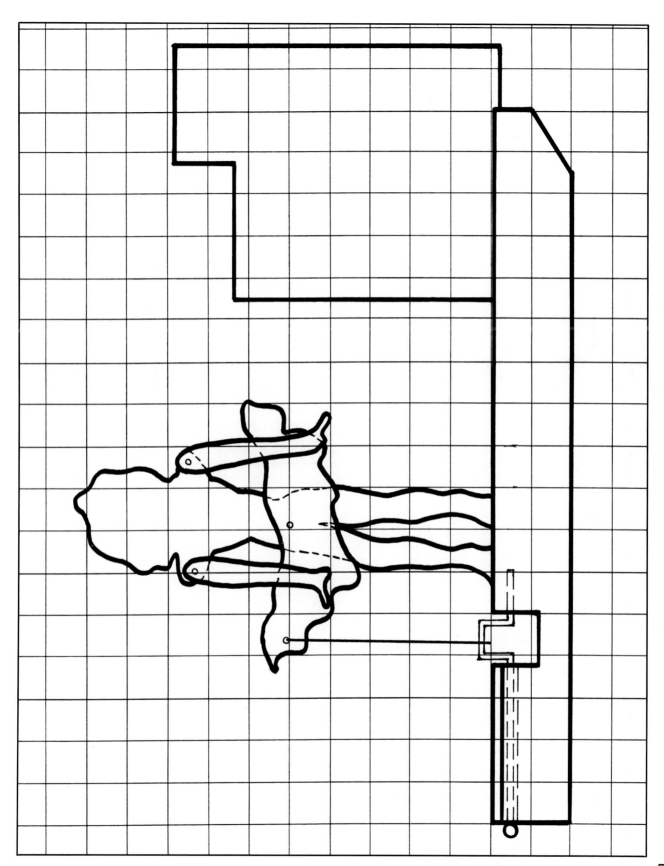

MARILYN'S WINDBLOWN SKIRT

Why should wind toys be limited to invoking the rural and historic? America's favorite fifties sex symbol—perched perilously on a pedestal in high heels over a Manhattan air vent in this scene from "The Seven Year Itch"— is assuredly as much a part of Americana as scarecrows or locomotives.

With a simple single-throw crankshaft, the standard split 1 x 1-1/2" base, and our usual 16-1/2" propeller, this project poses few new woodworking or mechanical challenges. Deciding which features best give away our screen star's identity, however, should give you room to explore characterization. Was it the blond hair, the coyly closed eyes, the plunging neckline, the diaphanous dress, or the heels that made Marilyn? Probably all of the above, but you settle on your own suite of features.

Marilyn's body is actually two pieces. First, a profile of her upper body and legs is cut from 1/2" plywood. Then the dress, in two outer panels, is rendered in 1/4" plywood. Her bosom is fixed to the shoulders, and the swinging arms go atop that.

The way this all works is that everything above her legs rocks on a wire-brad pivot inserted through a hole drilled at her belt buckle and into the 1/2" waist behind. As the connecting rod pushes up and tugs down on the end of her skirt, it waffles in the breeze. Her arms, though, are loosely suspended on wire brads that are tacked into her shoulders. Marilyn's arms hang vertically to restrain her skirt against the rising currents.

To keep Marilyn's propeller upwind, we added a 1/4" tail section and decorated it with a suitable backdrop. We just clipped a Manhattan skyline from a magazine ad, glued it to the wood, and protected it with a coating of clear finish.

You can add security to Marilyn and the Manhattan skyline by tacking them to the base that encloses the crankshaft rod before you install that piece. Just a couple of small nails set into her feet from below will make her existence far more stable.

This is one whirligig that may be more at home on a penthouse balcony than in a suburban backyard. But let's not limit ourselves. Cultural icons— whether they originate in Hollywood, Memphis or the Big Apple—can turn up anywhere the wind blows.

MODEL-T TUNE-UP

Once you've gotten comfortable making scrolled cuts with a saw and bending crankshafts, you might be ready to try pushing detail to the limit. If so, feel free to use Henry's famous Ford for inspiration. It's where we let out all the stops just to demonstrate what can be done with imagination, materials, and paint.

First the easy part: the body of our Model-T starts as a 1 x 6 that's 14-1/2" long. The seat, the convertible top, and even its pivot are all part of this board. The hood, down to the level of the crankshaft, however, is a separate piece. Use the grid diagram to duplicate our shape, or fashion the profile of your own favorite marque.

To form the see-through engine bay, start with a 1 x 2-3/8" x 2-7/8" rectangle, and cut the 1/8" x 1/8" crankshaft slot into it. Then drill holes large enough to accept your coping- or saber-saw blade at each corner so that they'll just touch the edge of the proposed opening—except at the top. Up there, center the holes on the line vertically so when you saw across you'll end up with hemispherical combustion chambers.

In auto engineering lingo, this engine design is perfectly square. The pistons are 3/8" dowel, and the crank throw is 3/8". For simplicity's sake, we decided to make pistons 1 and 4 fixed at top dead center, while 2 and 3 move up and down on a common crank throw. They slide on 1/16" brass wire.

Details, details: the radiator is a tiny brass cap nut. The windscreen is made of brass wire. The steering column is a length of 1/4" brass tube, with a 1/8"-thick, 1"-diameter steering wheel attached to the top with a sheet metal screw. Running lamps are 1/4" x 1/2" wooden blocks with ball-headed pins painted the color of brass. Moving to the rear, there's the 5/8" x 1-1/2" dowel fuel tank with brass nut for a cap. All the fenders are 1/8"-thick sawed on a bandsaw from 3/4" stock.

Then there are the wheels. The inner wheel—the black part—is a 1/4" x 3-1/4" disk made with a hole saw. The tire—the gray part—is 1/4" thick and glued to the inner wheel. We cut it by first cutting a 2-3/4" hole with the plywood clamped to another piece of stock. Then we used the same center with the 3-1/4" hole saw to yield a ring. The hub, too, is a separate piece: a 1/4"-thick 3/8" disk with a small hole in the center for a nail. The spokes consist of 1/8" dowels applied with glue. To attach them, stick another small disk of 1/4" material behind—to space the wheels out to match the fenders—and use glue and nails through the hub centers.

Out front, the radiator fan has a standard propeller hub but is only 12" in diameter—since not much torque is required to operate this lightweight roadster. Rather than rounding the blades, we cut them square to look more realistic.

Be sure to keep the mounting pivot point fairly far forward, since there is not a great deal of natural tail effect.

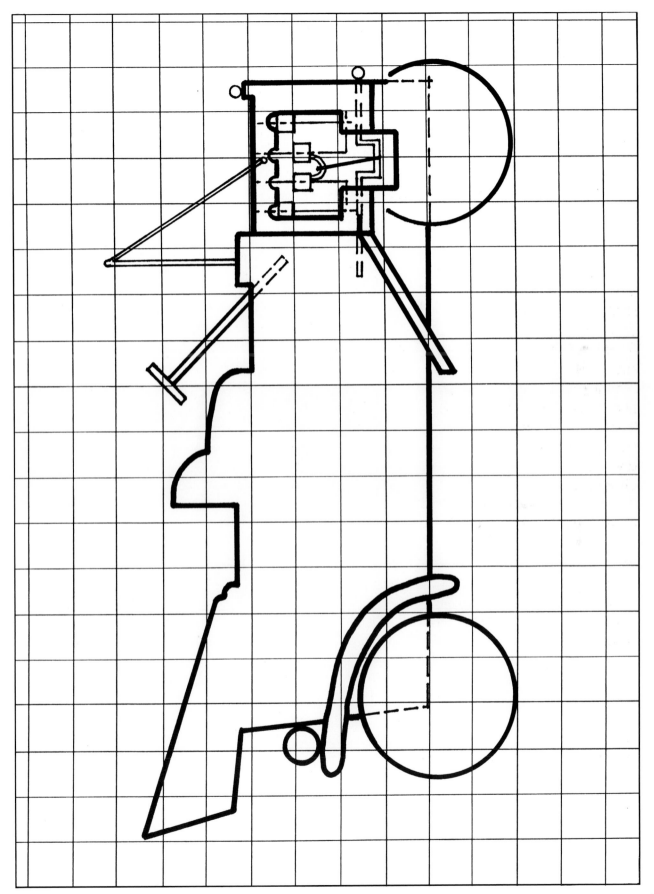

CANINE INTERVENTION

You might say that "Fido Express" is taking a big bite out of the Post Office in this whirligig. The eternal struggle between dogs and postal workers has been part of the American scene for generations, as our heroic mailman—presumably having triumphed over rain, sleet, snow, and gloom of night—is shown coming to an ignoble end at the teeth of his arch enemy.

Fido

CANINE INTERVENTION

Although this whirligig is powered by a simple crank, the interplay of the various pivots is complicated and must be "just so" for the postman's pants to slip off convincingly. Be prepared to experiment a bit with linkages and pivot points, as we did.

Notice, too, that the base of our photographed whirligig has a notch cut to accommodate the crank. You can use this method by simply following the procedure for notch-and-drive-shaft-channel construction detailed elsewhere in this book. (You could also position the driveshaft higher, through the doghouse, to avoid having a notch in the base.)

We fashioned the doghouse, mailman, and mailbox from 1/2" plywood. (If you have a dog, or even a favorite letter carrier, you may want to customize your design to suit.) The dog and the mailman's shorts are cut from 1/4" plywood.

The propeller is 16-1/2" in diameter and will be fastened to the threaded crankshaft in the usual manner. Of course, the shaft itself is a length of 1/8" welding rod.

We suggest you first paint the mailman, and use a thin wire brad pivot and washer to fasten his shorts in place. With that done, you can determine the best mounting point for the dog's rear feet—one that will allow the dog, by pivoting over a relatively short arc, to remove and replace the shorts. You may want to fashion a small 1/2" plywood tab to fasten to the base and use for mounting the dog's foot. You could also simply add a screw-eye at the appropriate point, and build the pivot out of a small bolt, nut, and washers.

With this much figured out, drill a drive-rod hole in the dog's tail and paint the whirligig. (You might find that, by experimenting with the 1/16" brass drive , you can avoid the complicated linkage shown in the photo.) When you're finished, you'll have one postal product that'll never be returned for insufficient fun!

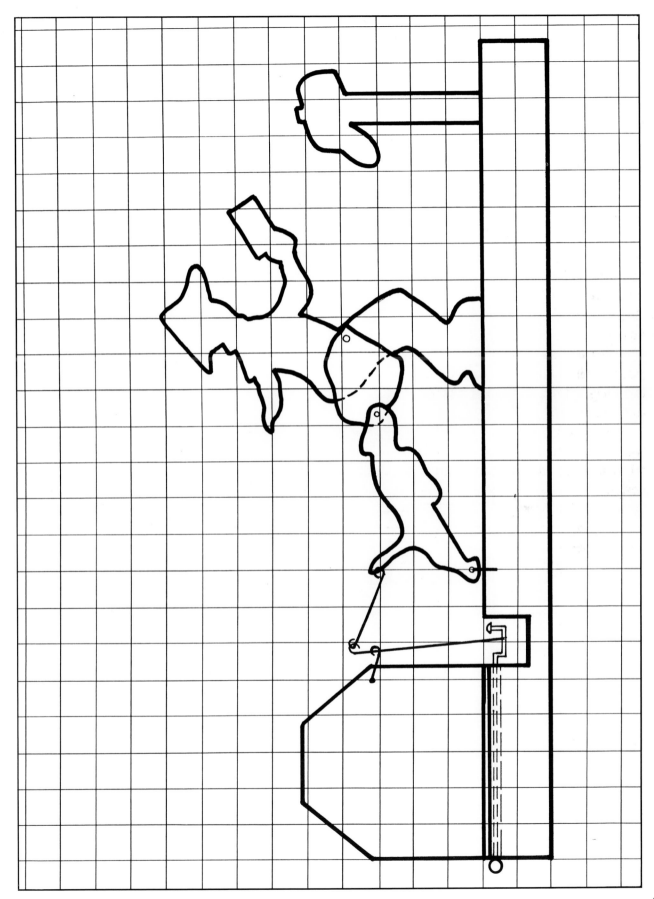

89

SPACE SHUTTLE

True, there is something a bit anachronistic about a space shuttle with a propeller. So in this design, the propeller simulates a fiery wake leeward behind the ship, while the bay doors open to expose its payload. NASA might not approve of this unauthorized appropriation of high technology, but we're sure they'll forgive as long as we stay in low orbit.

SPACE SHUTTLE

The base of this project follows much the same approach as others in this book. Start with a piece of solid lumber about 2 x 2-1/2" x 20". Lay the board on its side, and saw it in two lengthwise at a point 1-1/2" from one edge. Then saw the 1/8" x 1/8" groove for the crankshaft in the freshly cut face of the 1-1/2" piece.

Aside from the cargo bay doors and payload, all of the shuttle itself is made from 1x lumber: 1 x 10 for the body, and 1 x 8 for the wing. To prepare the body, start with a section of 1 x 10 that's 18" long, and pencil on the shape from our grid diagram. We suggest cutting the notches for the cargo doors and the wing after you've scrolled out the basic shape. The wing itself comes from an 8-1/2" piece of the 1 x 8. To get just the right cut-out profile on the body, use the edge of the 1 x 8 to guide your pencil.

The cargo bay doors are 1/4" x 1-3/4" x 4" plywood, but you can simply match them to your notch—whatever it may be. Use pairs of 3/4" hinges to attach them to the body. As for payload, we're into telescopes. But, if you've got a military bent, go ahead and fantasize about what star wars might look like.

This propeller demonstrates a different approach from our standard round hubs. It consists of a half-lapped cross of 3/4" x 3/4" x 7-1/2" stock, with 2"-deep notches for the 1/4" x 5-3/4" blades cut to place them only about 20° off the wind. The idea here is to cut down the prop's rotational speed, so the craft doesn't gyrate like a loose shingle in a stiff breeze. You can find the center of the hub for the crankshaft hole by drawing crossing diagonals.

Again, to keep motions from getting too wild, we bent in only a 1/2" throw into the 1/8" crankshaft. The crank goes in the 1/8" slot (along with some beeswax or soap for lubrication), the other half of the base gets glued and nailed back on, and the usual assortment of wooden beads and No.6-32 brass nuts keep things in place and spinning without binding.

The shuttle's landing gears consist of two 1-1/2" eye screws set into the underside of the wings 1-1/2" apart, to center the shuttle over the base. Woodscrews through the eyes—not quite tightened down—let the assembly rock. Eye screws and 1/16" welding rod connect the bay doors to the base, so the doors open and close as the shuttle moves up and down.

Unless you're feeling really fanciful, the space program has already chosen a color scheme for your shuttle. The propeller, though, offers opportunities as a non-standard part. We went for the "fade-away spiralling flame" look.

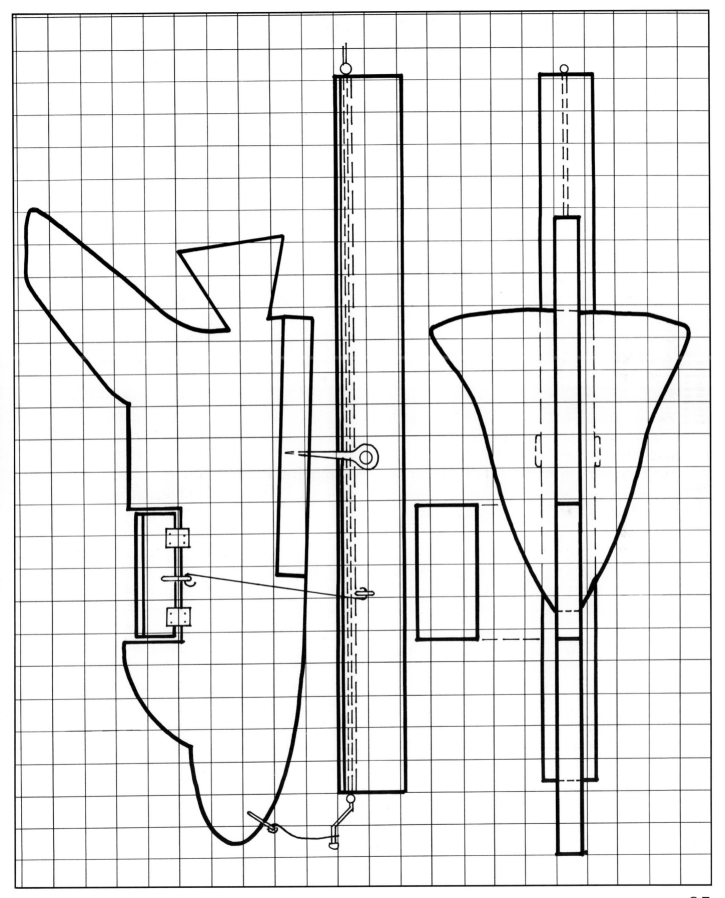

THE DUCK HUNTER

If you count an enthusiastic nimrod among your friends, this whirligig should make a well-appreciated gift. (Hint: the hunter can be customized in your friend's likeness, and positioned in a different environment, perhaps shooting at a flushing pheasant in a field, etc.) If they share our proficiency with a scatter gun, you'll find, as we did, that this whirligig is remarkably true to life: no matter how many times the hunter shoots, that bird just keeps on flying!

THE DUCK HUNTER

The base is a 2 x 1-1/2" x 19" piece of banak. Measure 12-1/4" from one end, and cut a 1-1/4" x 1-1/4" mortise, as shown. Now rip the 1/4" caps off the mortised surface. Then cut the 1/8" groove for the crank.

Next, cut a 24-3/4" length of 1/8" welding rod. Place it in the slot, with approximately 1-1/2" sticking out at the "propeller" end. Mark where the shaft enters the notch, then remove the rod and bend the 3/4" x 3/4" U-crank. Place the rod back in the slot, checking the fit, and mark a point 1/8" past where the shaft exits the slot at the far end of the base. Now remove the rod, form a 90° bend at the mark, measure 1-1/8" down, and complete the crank with another 90° bend.

The propeller is a standard 16-1/2"-diameter four-blader. It's mounted to the threaded crank with brass nuts, and incorporates wooden-bead bearings for easy movement. Install the crank, and glue the strips in place above it.

The hunter, water, boat, and marsh grass are all cut from 1/2" marine plywood. The duck's body and the hunter's arm/gun piece are cut from 1/4" plywood. The duck's spinning wings, and the small rectangles that connect each pair of wings and form their air foils, are cut from 1/8" plywood. Paint all of the pieces, except surfaces to be glued, before beginning to work on their assembly.

First, mark the pivot point of the arm/gun piece, drill an oversized hole through that piece, and then drive a wire-brad axle through the hole and into the hunter's shoulder. Then hold the marsh grass in position and mark the point at which the rod connecting the duck to the crank will have to pass through it. Drill a 1/16" hole to allow the rod to pass through. Then, working from the underside of the grass section, insert the drill bit and "wobble" it, creating a V-shaped hole that will accommodate the side to side play of the connecting rod.

Before gluing each pair of duck wings to a short rectangle of 1/8" stock, taper the ends of the wings into opposing air foils, effectively making a propeller. (To see this on a large scale, turn to the road runner and coyote designs.) Now drill an oversized hole through the body of the duck, then a second one into the bottom, to accept the mounting rod. Drive a wire brad through the center of one wing assembly, then slip it through the hole and drive it into the far wing assembly, leaving enough play to allow them to spin. Now the arm/gun can be fastened to the main crankshaft with a length of 1/16" brass rod.

And that's that—a wind-toy that will provide endless hours of entertainment, even if hunting itself isn't always all it's "quacked" up to be.

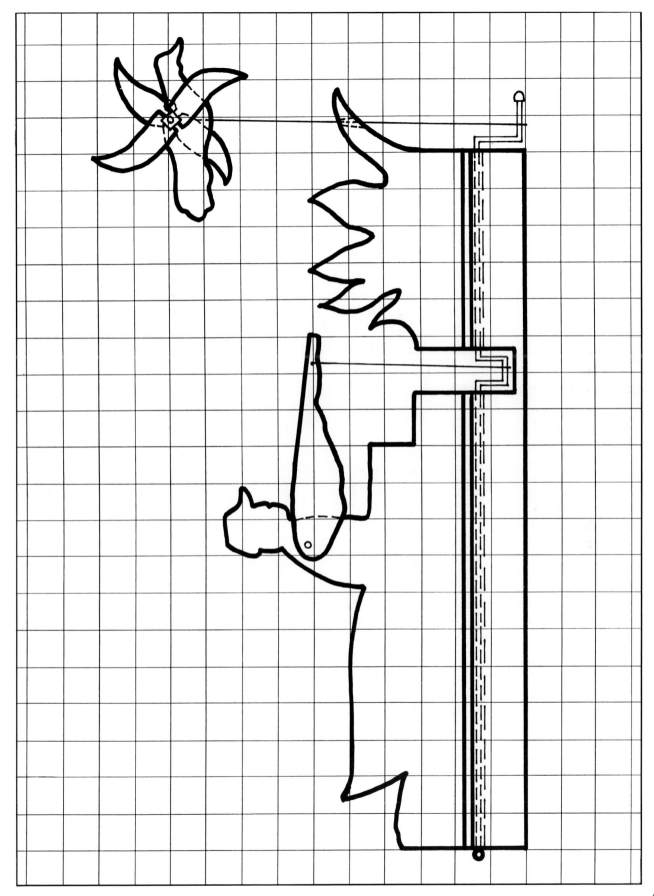

97

The visual joke of "the scarecrow that *doesn't*" probably goes back to the first gardener who tried to put a surrogate in charge of the crops, and learned that—at least where crows are concerned—the term "birdbrain" ought to be a compliment. Our own straw man carries on that fine old "corny" tradition, standing stoically, raising not a glove while the raven raiders cavort and caw amongst the cobs. And every time it looks like he just might get a bird in the hand, a trick of the wind will cause the feathered freebooter to fly just out of reach.

The base of this whirligig begins as a 2 x 2-1/2" x 22" piece of stock. First, cut the two 1-1/4" x 1-3/8" mortises. Once the mortises are cut, you'll want to rip a 1/4" strip from the mortised side of the board, producing three 1/4"-thick slats. Now run the 1/8" x 1/8" saw-kerf shaft channel along the cut surface of the base.

The crank begins as a 29"-long (approximately) piece of 1/8" welding rod. Place it in the slot, leaving about 1-1/2" overlapping at one end to mount the propeller. Now mark the beginning point for the first crank, remove the rod, form the crank, reinstall the rod in its shaft, and (if the fit is OK so far), mark and form the second crank. At this point, if the shaft fits and the cranks can move freely, you can mark the exposed ends of the crank, thread them with a No.6-32 die, and strip any extra off the rear end (which will only have to accept two brass nuts).

You can now make the propeller (our standard 16-1/2" diameter unit), and cut out the scarecrow (1/2" marine plywood), the cornstalks and haystack (1/4" plywood), and crows (1/4" plywood wings attached to carved 1/2"

dowel). If you're not using our patterns, do make sure the scarecrow's hands will match the span between the two cranks.

Mark the appropriate spots on the underside of the figure's hands, drill through with a 1/8" bit, and manipulate the drill to form a V-shaped slot that will allow for the sideways motion of the rods that move the crows.

Most of the assembly can be done with glue, though you might want to run some fine wire brads through the 1/4" base caps, from beneath, into pre-drilled holes in the bases of the cornstalks for security. The scarecrow is mounted to a short section of 1/4" dowel inserted into a 1" dowel base. The propeller is secured with a pair of brass nuts, using a wooden bead as a bearing.

Now run the crow support rods through the scarecrow's hands, bend them around the cranks, trim them to length, and insert their tops into the crows.

Depending on your paint job and siting, your finished whirligig could prove to be a real garden guardian, or mere buffoonery.

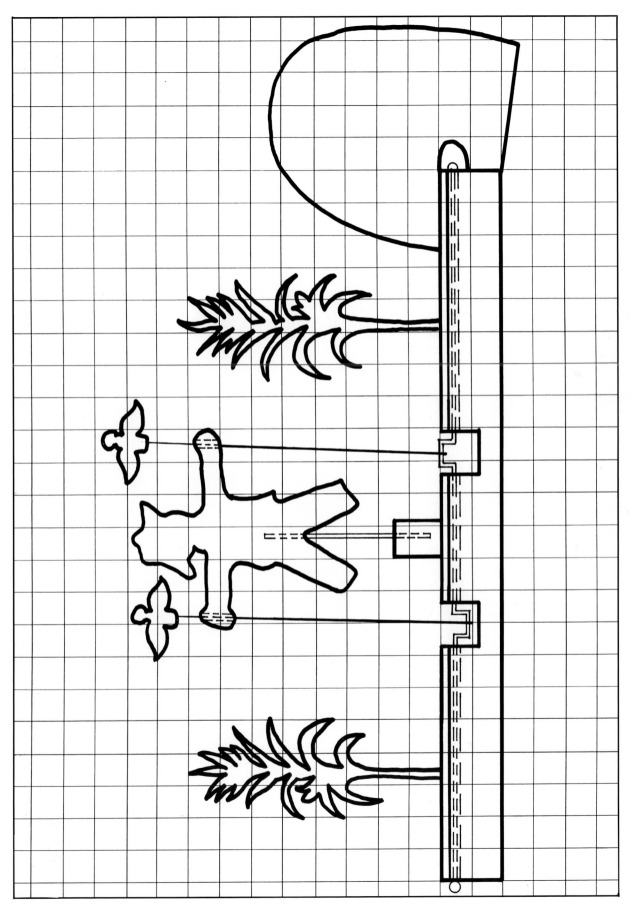

101

BREAKING GROUND

The sights and sounds of neighbors tilling gardens has, for many Americans, become as much a sign of Spring as the pussy willow. We're not sure how an infernal gasoline-driven device—one that seems designed to intensify the suffering of digging—achieved such status, but we can guarantee that employing this one will cause you no pain.

BREAKING GROUND

The base and crankshaft of this project present a wrinkle or two. Because we wanted both of our gardener's legs to pump , the two throws that control his feet and knees needed to be very close together. Our standard "bearing" system—consisting of ripping off a 1/4" strip of the 1x base, putting a groove in the base for the crankshaft, and fastening the strip back on—just wouldn't have given adequate support between those two adjacent throws.

Instead we mortised the base for both throws, ripped off the 1/4" strip (next to the fence), and bent a piece of rod into a U to go over the crank and into the narrow bearing surface between the close throws. The end of the crankshaft is inserted into a pre-drilled hole in the base (under the knees).

Our gardener's torso, head, and arm, as well as the fence, can be cut as one from 1/2" plywood. If you look closely, you'll see that this piece replaces the 1/4" crankshaft bearing cap where it connects to the base. His legs are 1/4" plywood and hinge on wire brads at his hips and knees. To provide additional support to those wobbly limbs, we attached the connecting rods at both his ankles and his knees. That way his lower legs are less prone to bow out when moving.

The tiller consists of a spool slotted with a fine saw. Cut-down pieces of tongue depressor or other thin stock is glued into the slots to form the blades.

You may need to raid an established sewer's basket to find the appropriate wooden spool, since these useful leftovers have now largely been replaced commercially by plastic. The control arms of the tiller are dowels drilled at both ends. The lower holes accommodate the tiller's brass-rod axle, while the upper ones are fixed to the gardener's hands by a smaller perpendicular dowel that acts as the tiller's handle.

The greenery that this ground-breaking device is perpetually ready to turn under is 1/4" plywood. A 1/4" groove is cut in the base to accept this panel.

Unlike many of the other whirligigs in this book, our gardener gets his impetus from a rear-mounted propeller—what aviators would call a "pusher prop." (This approach is worth considering anytime your proposed design won't conveniently include a fin to keep a forward-mounted prop pointed into the wind. Just set the pivot about two-thirds of the base length from the prop, and the assembly will always head up correctly.)

Should you take exception to gasoline-powered contraptions in your garden, consider adding large wheelplates to the ends of the spool, converting this roto-tiller to an old-fashioned push lawn mower. Or you could adapt our linkages to put a person with spade or fork into action. Be forewarned, though, that it could be a long row to hoe.

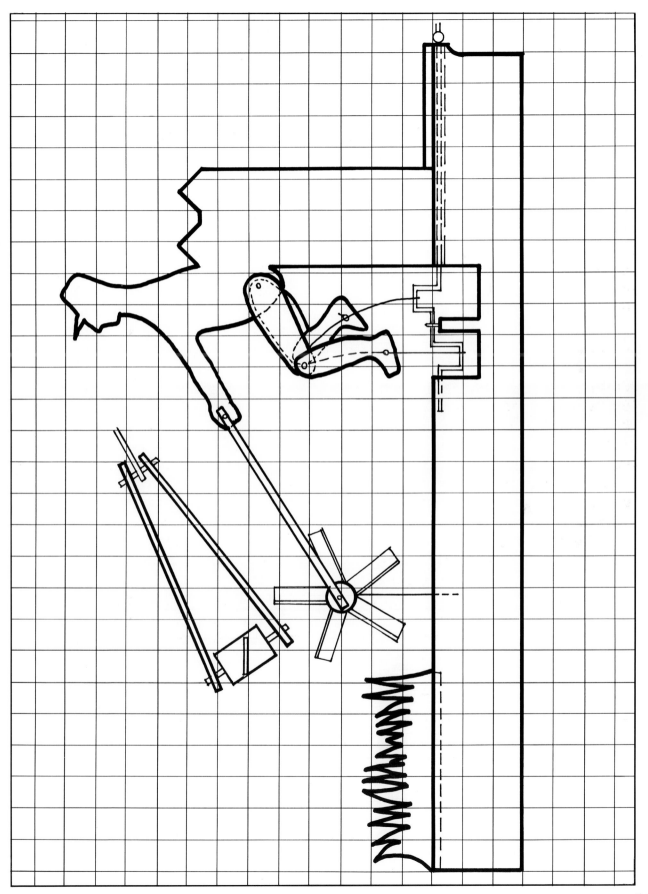

HALLOWEEN FANTASY

By tradition, this Sleepy Hollow trio is a celebration of "things that go bump in the night." Like many of the multiple-crank whirligigs in this collection, there's a lot happening here once the propeller starts spinning its magic, but the details needn't spook the journeyman wind-toy maker.

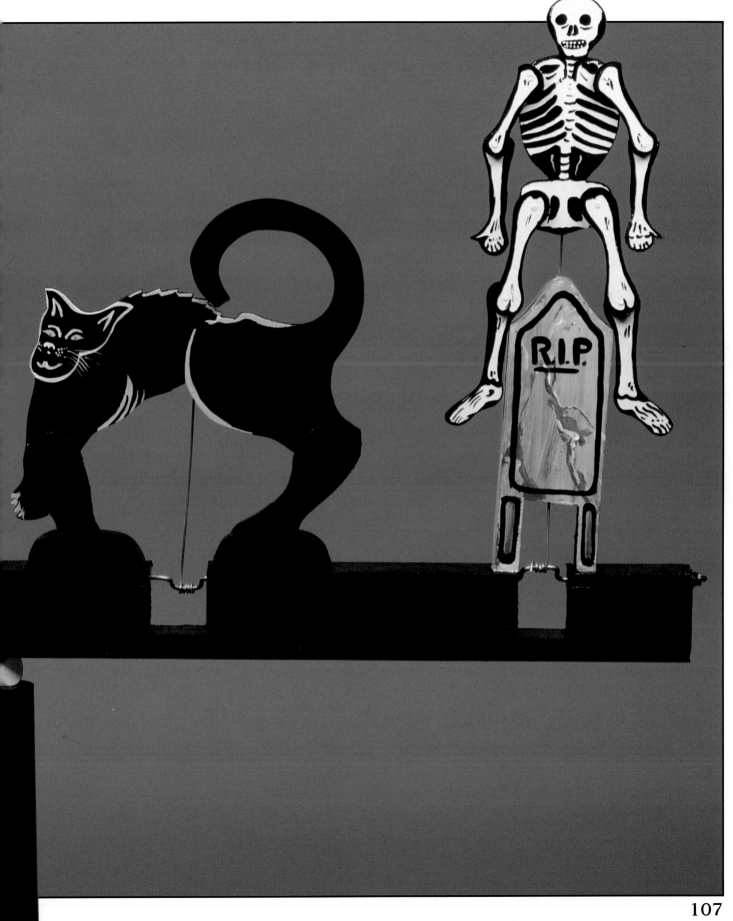

HALLOWEEN FANTASY

The base of this whirligig may be longer than usual, but is formed in the usual manner. First cut the notches, as indicated in the drawing, then rip across the top to produce the four 1/4"-thick slats. With that done, run the standard 1/8" x 1/8" saw kerf across the top of the base to house the drive shaft.

The propeller--16-1/2" in diameter—can be assembled at any time and set aside. We painted ours orange...though a thorough night-time effect could be created by painting the prop and base black, and using phosphorescent highlights on the moving figures.

The bottom of the pumpkin and the tombstone are 3/4" stock. The pumpkin's top and the torso of the skeleton are 1/2", while the skeleton's limbs and the cat are 1/4" plywood. The two bases for the cat's feet are 3/4" solid stock with 1/4" grooves cut in their tops to support the 1/4" limbs that pivot.

Next, mark the center point on the base of the pumpkin and tombstone and drill 1/8" holes through these pieces, wobbling the drill as you finish to produce V-shaped openings that are wider at the bottom to allow for the sideways play of the push rods. Now you can mark the various pivot points and drill the necessary holes; then go on to paint each part in ghoulish detail.

While the paint is drying, measure, form, and fit the drive shaft, lubricating it with soap or wax when it's finished. You can then cover the installed shaft with the pre-cut and painted 1/4" slats.

Drill 1/8" holes part way into the pumpkin bottom's sides, and all the way through its top sides, to accommodate the 1/8" brass guide-rods that support the top half. Now drill a 1/16" hole from the bottom center of the upper half of the pumpkin, extending an inch or so into the figure. Glue a too-long piece of 1/16" brass rod into the hole, then run the remainder down through the base of the pumpkin, measure to the throw of the crank, trim the rod, and fasten it in place.

Go on to assemble the other figures with wire-brad pivots; then measure and secure the 1/16" drive rod for the cat. For the skeleton, pre-drill a 1/16" hole for the brass push-rod, insert through the tombstone and attach it the same as the pumpkin.

Finally, secure the propeller to the threaded drive shaft with brass nuts, place another pair on the rear end of the shaft to secure it in place, and install the whirligig in your front yard on a moonlit night. It should serve as a special treat for your little trick-or-treaters!

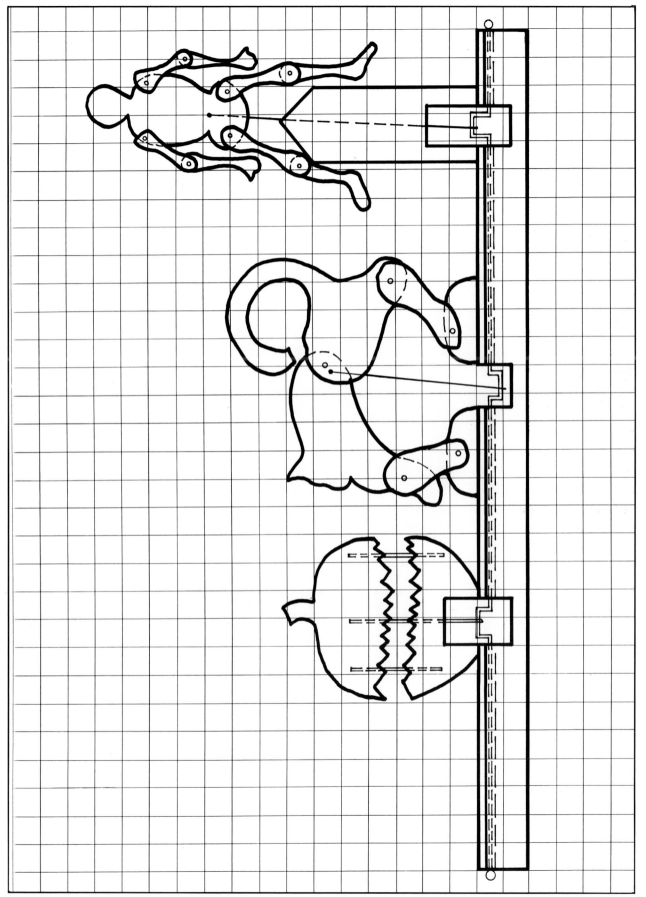

I LOVE A PARADE

While we're not about to claim that the great American institution, the parade, is near the verge of extinction, it can be hard to find one of your own. The only way we know to guarantee yourself a gala fest—whether it's for a birthday, a holiday, or the first robin of spring—is to build your own.

Here's an example of what can happen when you take a relatively straightforward three-throw linkage and let your imagination run free.

The base is a simple piece of 2 x 2-1/2" stock 21-1/2" long. To prepare the notches for the crank throws, cut three mortises across it that are 1-1/4" wide and 1-3/8" deep.

To prepare the crank, start with a piece of 1/8" welding rod about 30" long. Form 3/4" throws 3/4" wide with locking-jaw pliers, as described in the chapter on assembly. The push rods are 1/16" brass that loop through tiny brass eye screws on each figure.

It's probably easiest to install all the mechanical components except the propeller and lock nuts before installing the crank in the base. Once the shaft is ready, apply a little soap or beeswax to the groove in the base for lubrication, set the crank into the groove, and glue and nail the 1/4"-thick cap pieces atop the assembly. A standard 16-1/2" diameter propeller will start the band marching.

Rather than provide you with painstaking detail of the figures themselves, we'd prefer to give you the general parameters in which we worked (and the grid diagram, of course) and let your imagination take over. You may, however, find it easier to increase the scale slightly.

Starting from the front, our majorette is, like all the other figures, cut from 1/2" plywood. Her baton—which is actually a propeller that spins—consists of a length of 1/8" dowel with 1/8" blades glued to each end at opposing angles. The axle is a wire brad through a hole drilled in the baton shaft. (This is very detailed work that would be much easier at larger scale.)

The flag bearer holds a 3/16"-diameter pole with the 1/8" flag glued on. His 1/8"-thick arm pivots at the shoulder on a wire brad with a brass washer between the arm and the body. The arms on the trombonist and the bass drummer are done in the same way. Likewise, their instruments are 1/8" thick.

Each figure is glued to the base at two points. Even so, a little extra security helps. You can form small pins by tacking nails into the base where the feet will go and cutting the heads off about 1/4" up with wire cutters. Then drill shallow lead holes in the feet of the figures for them to settle onto the nails. Of course, screws or nails offer even more security. Again, pre-drill the holes first.

Colors? Red, gold, and black appealed to us. But you have your own alma mater, so be true to your school.

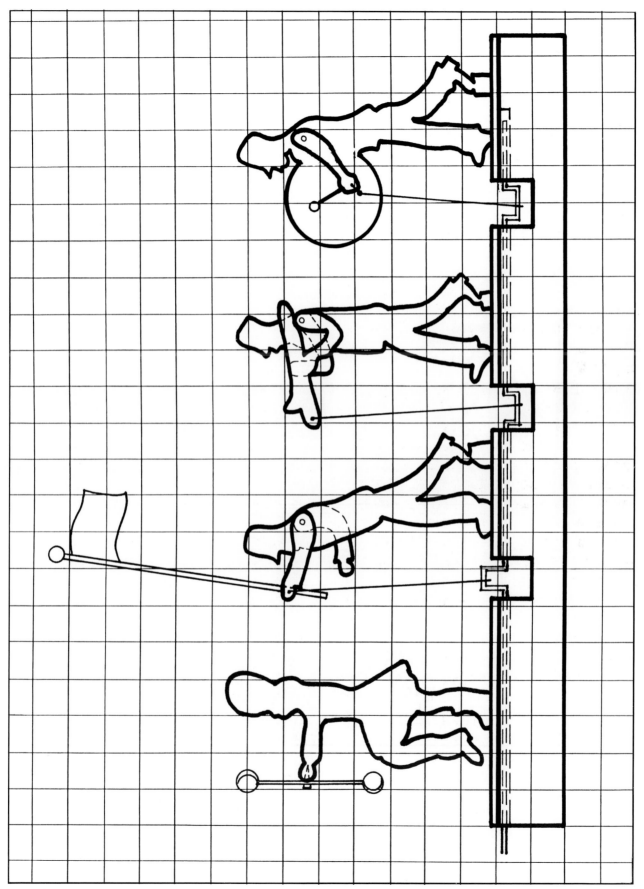

113

RUNNIN' AGAINST THE WIND

Yeah, the winds of time have
scattered most of the classic rock bands
of the late sixties (although the Stones just keep on
rollin', and the Dead won't stay buried). Our whirligig,
then, serves as a memorial to those heady days when any
kid who could afford a Fender guitar could climb the
stairway to stardom with their own garage band.
The music may have been crude and raucous,
but you couldn't beat the dream...

RUNNIN' AGAINST THE WIND

Although it includes notches for four separate cranks, this whirligig's base is constructed in the same manner as are the simpler pedestals used in our other designs. Cut the notches as indicated, smoothing their bottoms if necessary; rip 1/4" slats from the top of the base; and then run the 1/8" x 1/8" saw kerf along the top to accommodate the four-crank drive shaft.

Construction of the shaft, too, follows that described for simpler drives. Begin with a 34-1/2"-long section of 1/8" welding rod, and place it in the groove, allowing 1-1/2" overhang on the propeller end. Then, one at a time, mark the leading edge of the notches, bend the 3/4" x 3/4" cranks, try the fit, and go on to the next notch. (Don't worry if the shaft ends up a little short; its rear end will be hidden beneath the cap at the back of the whirligig.)

The band figures themselves are cut out in sections. The lower bodies and the backing for the drums are fashioned from 1/2" marine plywood, while the upper bodies, arms, and amplifier are cut from 1/4" plywood. The drums shown in relief are made from small sections of ripped dowel and pieces of half-round molding; the head of the microphone is cut from a sanded-to-shape dowel. The propeller is the standard four-bladed 16-1/2"-diameter model.

The pivots for arms and torsoes are pre-drilled, then joined with fine wire brads (or small brass wood screws). The propeller is secured with twin brass nuts, and the rear end of the shaft simply covered with the appropriate piece of 1/4" slat. (Before securing the shaft cover, you might want to drive brads through it from beneath to fit into pre-drilled holes in the bases of the figures for additional security.)

Now drill the 1/16" holes where the drive rods fasten to the moving parts, glue the figures in place, and connect the 1/16" brass rods to the crankshafts. You can wrap the microphone rod through an eye screw in the lead singer's hand, so the crank will rock the singer back and forth as the microphone moves up and down.

Consider our paint scheme only as a general suggestion. Why not dig through your old albums for inspiration? (After all, don't such classics as the Swingin' Blue Jeans deserve a taste of immortality? No? Then how about Blue Cheer? Mother Earth? Left Bank?)

That's all there is to it.
God knows, it's only rock'n'roll.
But we like it.

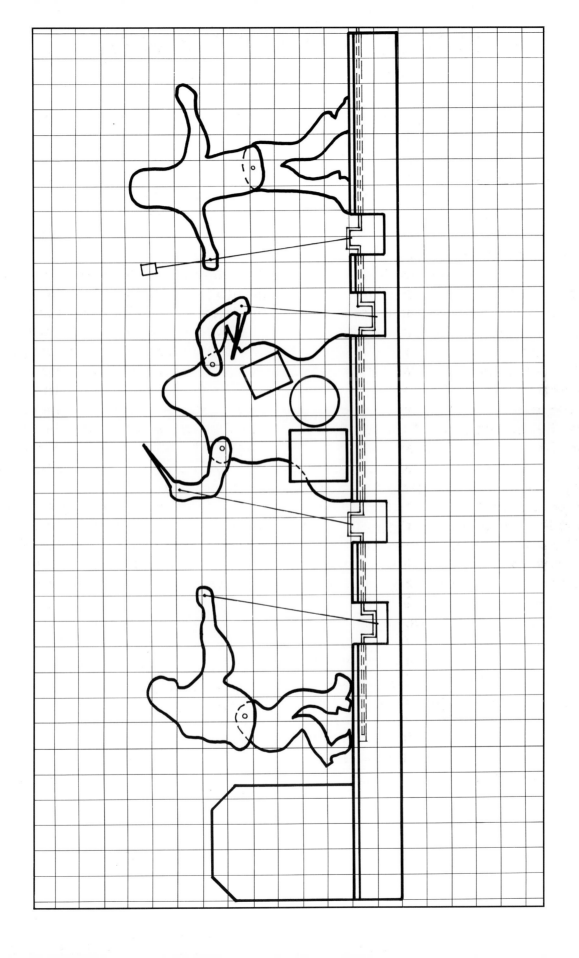

117

FROGS OF CALAVERAS COUNTY

Frogs? Plural? Okay, you Twain fanatics took one look at the photo and realized that Mark's ambitious amphibian seems to have reproduced. But maybe you didn't know that Calaveras County's patriarchs, perhaps recognizing a good hyperbole when it jumped in front of them, have now established a frog-jumping contest as an annual event. Our frogs may not establish distance records, but you'll have a hard time finding five others that will dance as dependably in rhythm.

Start with a piece of straight-grained 2 x 4 that's 29 inches long. On one end, cut a 1/4"-wide, 2-1/2"-deep notch to receive the tail fin. Then lay the board on its side and rip it in two at a point 2" from one edge. Take the 2"-wide piece and rip a 1/8"-wide, 1/8" deep groove for the crankshaft in the face you just sawed.

Use the grid diagram to position the 7/8"-deep mortises, so the openings will be split equally vertically between the two halves. A tablesaw dado will make preparing the mortises easier, but you can certainly do an equally good job with a handsaw and a chisel.

The upper half of the base piece needs a little extra work. Since the connecting rods that support the frogs will be moving side-to-side slightly as the go up and down, the holes for the rods really need to be slots—or rather, a hole at the top that becomes a slot as you get closer to the crank. You can do this easily enough with an electric drill. Start from the top and drill one hole at an angle. Then, starting from the same hole, force the bit in at the complementary opposite angle. Then "hog out" the material between these two holes.

The tail, which is needed to keep our froggies' faces perpendicular to the wind, is made from 1/4" plywood. Follow our cutting profile, or freehand your own—a big webbed foot, for example. You may want to end your crankshaft 1" after the last bend, or secure it externally with lock nuts as we have done.

Frogs are formed from 3/8"-thick plywood or solid stock (we used mahogany). If you'll look carefully, you'll notice we really have only two styles. Frogs three and five are simply mirror images.

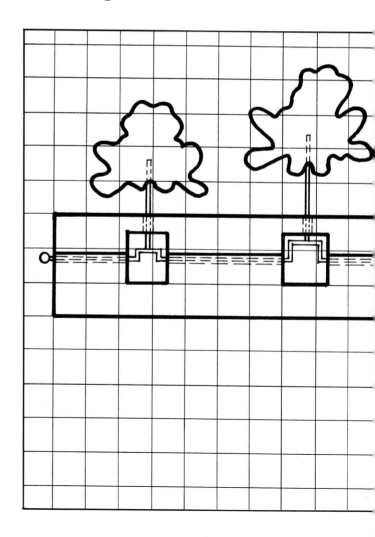

The propeller is just the standard 16-1/2"-diameter item with webbed feed painted on. The blades could have been actually cut in the shape of feet, but only if stacked and cut all at once so that they would balance.

To keep the frogs in non-monotonous motion, spread their crank throws around the crank's revolution. The width and depth of all our crank throws is 3/4". However, to achieve different jumping heights, the depth of throw can be varied slightly so long as the sideways motion does not become extreme.

Because the frogs are fairly stout and otherwise unsupported, we used 1/8" rod for their connecting rods as well. To attach them, we just drilled a 3/32" hole in each frog to force the connecting rod into.

But before you do that, spend a little time blending your green, black, and white paints to achieve frog likenesses. Whether princely or with a Kermit-like turn, they set the tone.

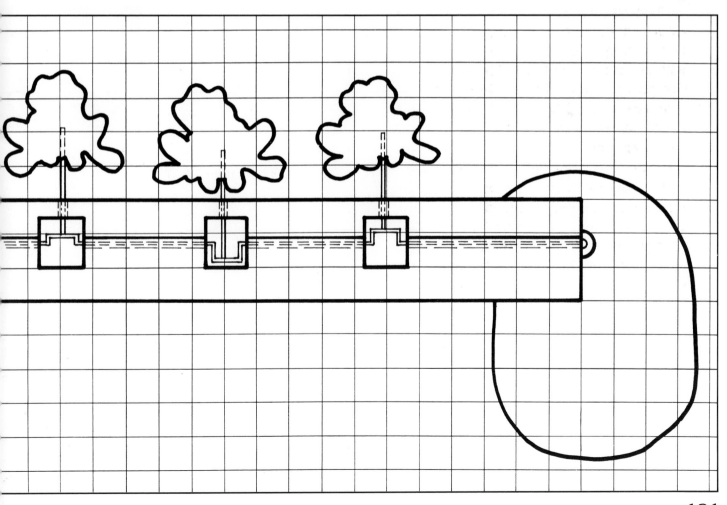

CAT HOUSE
ON A
FRIDAY NIGHT

What the heck. If Hollywood can make a mass-distribution film called "The Best Little Whore House in Texas," why shouldn't we further encourage the removal of the brothel from the ranks of taboo? After all, but for a few tax-troubled Nevada establishments, the "cat house" has passed the way of the drive-in movie theater. It seems that Americans have a much easier time cherishing those of questionable character—people or institutions—once they're dead.

CAT HOUSE ON A FRIDAY NIGHT

While the base and propeller of this whirligig follow much the same pattern as other projects in this book, the action parts are unique. All the goings-on inside the building take place in a 1/4" plywood sandwich—within which they slide up and down or pivot. There are any number of themes that could be developed along the same lines. A police or fire station, for instance, would be interesting and less prurient. So if you're not ready for neighborly comments about this yard decoration, use your imagination to develop another.

Without going into graphic detail about the action in this project, let us at least point out how the mechanisms work. Starting from the front, our 1/4"-thick arresting officer is about to announce his presence with a less-than-subtle baton tap on the door. His foot is anchored firmly to the steps, while his arm pivots at the shoulder.

On the first floor, someone's pulling down the window shade, unaware of the constable's imminent arrival. The arm and blind are one piece of 1/4" ply linked to the crank below and our Madame's hand above. She pivots at the hip just behind the right side of the window casing. You'll notice that this motion isn't entirely linear, but the small side-to-side movement she and our "john" introduce is well within the flexibility of the 1/16" brass connecting rod. Also, note the pairs of sandwiched shims in the pattern drawing that guide all the vertical motion.

We suggest that you keep the crank throws for the left and right window scenes 180° apart. Not only will it improve the action, but it will also ease the load on the propeller by having one set go up while the other comes down.

Moving toward the back door, downstairs, note that only the pants go up and down. Moon, as we like to call him, has each of his arms glued to the plywood house. A tiny eye screw in his back keeps the connecting rod running straight upward—to attach to the groping hands of the clientele.

Out back, though, one potential jail bird has gotten the word and has chosen to flee—*sans* shirt and slacks—in his boxers.

Visually, this project seems to demand a little different treatment than most others. With the comparatively large flat areas of plywood wall and the two-dimensional presentation, we didn't think that paint alone would be effective. Though it's still basically a profile, the windowsills and second-story fascia made from 1/4" plywood give it a bit more relief. The sloping roof helps out as well. Of course, it could be that were just picking nits. Maybe observers' attentions won't even focus on the roofline.

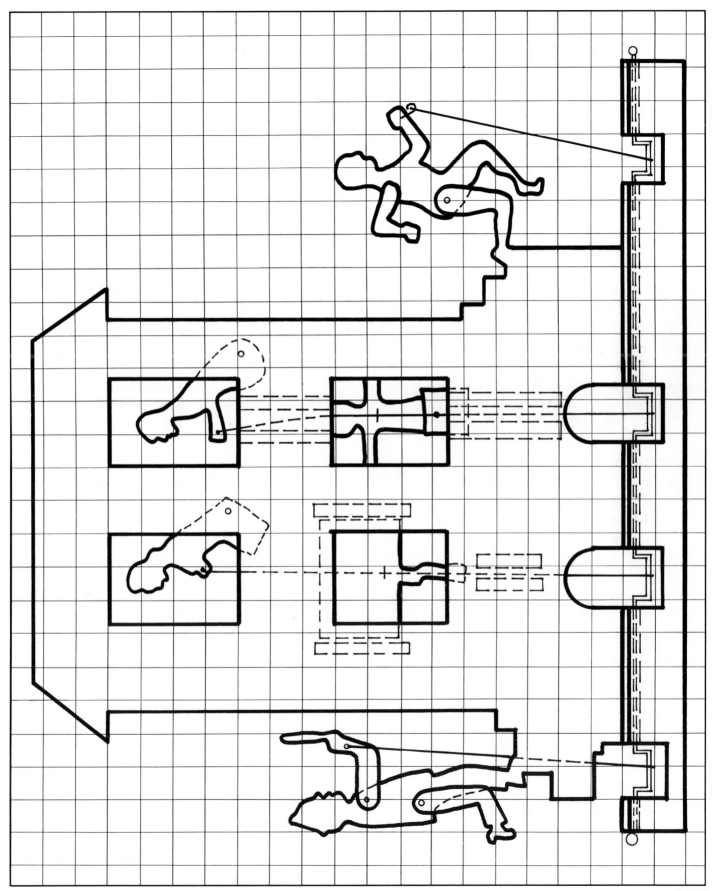

"Bicycle" whirligig
by Ed Smith,
Conover, North Carolina

CREDITS

Whirligig Designs
Thom Boswell: pgs. 40-125

Whirligig Makers
Claudia & Don Osby: pgs. 42, 44, 46, 50, 53, 60, 64, 82, 94, 98, 110, 118; Mark Dockery: pgs. 72, 76, 79, 86, 102, 106, 114, 122; Wayne Riddick: pgs. 40, 56, 68; Ralph Schmidt: p. 90

Whirligig Painters
Claudia Osby: pgs. 42, 44, 46, 50, 53, 60, 64, 72, 82, 86, 94, 98, 102, 110, 118, 122; Tim West: pgs. 40, 56, 68, 76, 79, 106, 114; Ralph Schmidt: p. 90

Additional Photography
Randy Sewell: pgs. 6 (top), 18, 19 (bottom right), 24, 25; Woody Bousquet: pgs. 19 (bottom left), 26, 27, 127; Dave Stuebner & Roger Hagerty: pgs. 20, 21; Rickey Yanaura: p. 17

Special Thanks
John Cram, New Morning Gallery, Asheville, NC; Georgine Clarke, Kentuck Center, Northport, AL; Andrew Glasgow, Folk Arts Center, Asheville, NC; Woody Bousquet, Warren Wilson College, Swannanoa, NC; Randy Sewell, Atlanta, GA

AUTHORS

David Schoonmaker and Bruce Woods have been collaborating on various publishing projects for more than 15 years. After working together on four magazines, their avocational interests in woodworking and the outdoors led them to co-author books. *Whirligigs and Weathervanes* is their second title, their first being *The Bird House Book*, which was also published by Sterling/Lark in 1991.

Currently, Woods is editor of *Writer's Digest* magazine, while Schoonmaker edits for Rodale Press. New projects are constantly hatching, and no one would be surprised if their names appeared together again soon.

Whirligigs by Vollis Simpson

INDEX